P9-CDE-687

THE MEANING OF BELIEF

THE MEANING OF BELIEF

Religion from an Atheist's Point of View

TIM CRANE

Harvard University Press

Cambridge, Massachusetts
London, England
2017

Copyright © 2017 by the President and
Fellows of Harvard College
All rights reserved
Printed in the United States of America

Third printing

Library of Congress Cataloging-in-Publication Data
Names: Crane, Tim, author.
Title: The meaning of belief : religion from an atheist's
point of view / Tim Crane.
Description: Cambridge, Massachusetts : Harvard
University Press, 2017. | Includes bibliographical
references and index.
Identifiers: LCCN 2017014817 | ISBN 9780674088832
(alk. paper)
Subjects: LCSH: Belief and doubt. | Atheists—Attitudes. |
Faith. | Psychology, Religious. | Religious adherents.
Classification: LCC BD215 .C823 2017 | DDC 202/.2—dc23
LC record available at https://lccn.loc.gov/2017014817

To my parents

Contents

Preface

As its title says, this book is concerned with the meaning of religious belief rather than its truth. So, unlike many recent contributions to the current public debate on religion, it will not discuss in any great detail the truth or falsehood of particular forms of atheism or theism. Nor will it attempt, as some recent atheist books have done, to identify the good bits in religious belief and sanitize them for atheistical purposes. Rather, the book's aim is to discuss what, in the broadest possible sense, religion means to people and what intellectual, ethical, and practical attitudes atheists themselves should take toward the phenomenon of religion and toward those who are religious.

Many recent atheist writers (especially the so-called New Atheists: Richard Dawkins, Daniel C. Dennett, A. C. Grayling, Sam Harris, and the late Christopher Hitchens) have taken an explicitly combative attitude to religion. Their writings are dominated by two views: (1) that religion is largely constituted by certain cosmological beliefs, none of which are true; and (2) that the proper atheistic attitude to religion should be to use scientific evidence and philosophical arguments to remove these beliefs and, with them, the phenomenon of religion itself.

In this book I argue that both of these views are mistaken. Against the first, I argue that although religion tends to involve an explicit cosmological element, this is not the totality of the religious worldview. This worldview should rather be seen as a combination of two fundamental attitudes. One is what I call the "religious impulse": a sense of the transcendent, of there being "more to it all than just this." The other is an attitude toward other people that I call "identification": belonging to a historical tradition, and making sense of the world through ritual and custom as an expression of this tradition. (This includes the moral element in religious belief too.) The link between these two attitudes is given by the idea of the sacred, in a way I explain in Chapter 3.

Against the New Atheists' second view, I claim that given the actual nature of religion, scientific and philosophical arguments are unlikely to be generally effective in eliminating religious belief. They may work in some limited contexts, but in most interactions they are useless—and this fact tells us something important about religion itself. It is massively improbable that religion will ever be removed from human societies as they actually are. So atheists have to find a more realistic and feasible way to relate to religion and the religious.

In place of the New Atheists' approach, I argue that we atheists should attempt to understand religion, and that we should attempt to tolerate it—within limits. We should try to understand religion because without such an understanding we lack an adequate sense of a fundamental part of human civilization and its history, and we therefore lack a proper understanding of ourselves. Understanding does not mean acceptance, and it does not necessarily mean respect. I don't say that all religious views are worthy of respect, but I do claim that we should tolerate them, so long as they fall within the rule of law. Toleration implies that one objects to what is being tolerated, not that one respects or admires it. So the reason atheists should tolerate religious views is not because they respect them, but because they should find a way of living in peace with the religious, rather than supposing that the phenomenon of religion will simply vanish in the face of rational or scientific argument.

This book is intended as a contribution to a public debate about an important issue. It is not supposed to be an academic work, or a piece of theology or anthropology; I offer no new theories or empirical discoveries. What I do offer is a philosophical picture of a real phenomenon, plus some practical advice to atheists. Chapter 1 outlines the basic ideas of religion, atheism, and belief that I will develop; Chapter 2 describes the cosmological content of religion, painting a very different picture from that of the New Atheists; Chapter 3 describes identification; Chapter 4 addresses the vexed question of the connection between religion and violence, and offers some reflections on whether religious belief is necessarily "irrational"; and Chapter 5 is about the attitude of tolerance that I recommend to nonbelievers.

My ideas for this book began to grow when I was asked to give the Bentham Lecture at University College London (UCL) in November 2007. The Bentham Lecture is a regular event sponsored by the UCL Philosophy Department and the British Humanist Association (BHA). Here I would like to thank Jo Wolff of UCL and Peter Cave of the BHA for the invitation to give the lecture. In my lecture I took the opportunity to criticize some aspects of contemporary humanism in the United Kingdom: its tendency to see itself as an alternative to a religion as a worldview; its exaggeration of the role played by religion as the cause of the world's problems; its insistence that religion is irrational and not merely false; and its exaggeration of the importance of cosmological belief, both as a part of religion and as part of the response to it. I argued that atheists should be trying to achieve what John Gray calls "a type of toleration whose goal is not truth but peace."[1]

My lecture went down very badly with its chosen audience, which was probably expecting yet another attack on the evils of religion. This response confirmed my suspicion, however, that there is room for another, somewhat different, atheist attitude to religion, and this book is the result.

Conversations with David Owens over the years have helped me greatly to work out my views on these questions. I would also like to thank Philip Goff, Stephen Hampton, Tom Pink, Rupert Shortt, and Michael Thorne for insights gained in various discussions, and I would like to acknowledge here the influence of the writings of Karen Armstrong, Thomas Nagel, and (especially) Roger Scruton. Philip Kitcher and an anonymous referee read the manuscript for Harvard University Press and generously offered many useful suggestions for improvement, which I have tried to accommodate in the final version. My wife, Kati Farkas, provided detailed and insightful comments that helped me enormously in revising the manuscript. My editor at Harvard, Ian Malcolm, has been unfailingly supportive and patient, and has shown his characteristic good judgment. Finally, I would like to thank my parents, Ann and Walter Crane, with whom I have been discussing these matters for years. My hope is to have written a book that they might like to read.

THE MEANING OF BELIEF

1

Religion and the Atheist's Point of View

When Pope Francis visited the Philippines in January 2015, his final mass in Manila attracted an audience of between 6 and 7 million people. In the same year, 2 million Muslims made the obligatory annual hajj pilgrimage to Mecca, spending over $8 billion during the period. These numbers are dwarfed, however, by the 26 million Shia Muslims who traveled to Karbala in Iraq in 2015 in the Arba'een pilgrimage to commemorate the death of Husayn ibn Ali, the Prophet Muhammad's grandson. Twenty-six million people: that's five times the population of Denmark. Two years earlier, 120 million people attended the Kumbh Mela Hindu festival at Allahabad, in the Uttar Pradesh province of India. On one day during this festival, an estimated 25 million people took part in ritual bathing at the confluence of the Ganges and Yamuna Rivers. These events, all happening within the last few years, are some of the largest single temporary gatherings of people ever recorded.

The numbers are staggering, and they give a snapshot of the extent of religious affiliation in the world today. According to the Pew Research Center, there are currently 2.2 billion Christians, 1.6 billion Muslims, and 1 billion Hindus worldwide.[1] Adherents of these three vast religions make up 4.8 billion of the world's 7.16 billion people. And then there are all the "smaller" religions: Judaism, Buddhism, Shinto, Jainism, Sikhism, and many others. Around 1.1 billion people identify as secular, atheist, agnostic, or nonreligious. Approximately 6 billion people, then, identify as belonging to one religion or another—over 80 percent of the world's population.

What is religion, and why does it move people? An impossibly large question, to be sure, especially for one person to answer in a single book.

However, impossibly large questions are the business of philosophy—what is goodness? what can we know? what is reality? how should we live?—and philosophy would be nothing if it did not try to answer such questions. So it is in this optimistic spirit that I approach this one.

This book is written from an atheist point of view, but it differs from some recent atheist writings on religion in two ways. First, it is not about the truth of religious belief but about its meaning: what it means to believe in religious ideas, what it means for believers, and what it should mean for nonbelievers too. It aims to be about the nature and meaning of religious belief in general; it does not make any contribution to the discussion of any specific doctrines of any specific religious faith or tradition. Second, it differs from much recent atheism in the picture of religion it draws. Contemporary atheist accounts tend to present religion as a kind of primitive cosmology—a primitive or proto-scientific theory of the universe as a whole—or as simply a moral code, or as some combination of these two things. While I think there are both cosmological and moral elements in religious belief, I reject the reduction of religious belief to either of them, or even to their combination. Religious belief is not simply a cosmology or simply a morality, and it is not simply a cosmology-plus-morality. We will fail to understand this fundamental human phenomenon if we try to force it into these preconceived categories.

The reader may press me to define what I mean by religion. In a strict sense of "definition," this probably can't be done. Friedrich Nietzsche said that only that which has no history can be defined, and if he is right (which he surely is), then religion cannot be defined.[2] For religion is so wrapped up with human history and prehistory that we should not hope for a sharp definition of the kind that we get in mathematics, for example, the paradigm of a subject matter (numbers, functions, sets, and so on) without a history. Rather than looking for a strict definition, we should seek "an understanding of religions by following the way they developed historically"—in Émile Durkheim's words.[3]

Most large-scale attempts to define religion will encounter some counterexample, in the sense that a religion can be found to which the definition does not apply, or that we will find something to which it applies that is not a religion. This is one reason that it has become almost a commonplace among those who theorize about religion that it is impossible to be defined. In his classic work, *The Varieties of Religious Experience,* William James comments on the variety of definitions in circulation and concludes that "the very fact that these definitions are so many and so different from one another is enough to prove that the word 'religion' cannot stand for any single principle or essence."[4] Some recent writers agree. Karen Armstrong observes that "there is no universal way to define religion" and argues that the concept itself is not obviously one that would have been recognized by more ancient societies: there is no single word in ancient Greek or Latin, nor in the Hebrew Bible, that we can translate as "religion."[5] In fact, the origin of the concept of the religious, as something opposed to the secular, is a matter of controversy and still somewhat obscure.

Nonetheless, if we are going to get a proper overview of our subject matter, we should try to specify as precisely as we can what it is we are talking about, even if we cannot answer the question of the historical origin of the concept, and even if what we come up with doesn't amount to anything like a rigorous mathematical definition (after all, very few things do). James had the right approach: "Let us rather admit freely at the outset that we may very likely find no one essence, but many characters which may alternately be equally important in religion."[6] So I will start with my first attempt to identify these characters.

Religion, as I am using the word, is a systematic and practical attempt by human beings to find meaning in the world and their place in it, in terms of their relationship to something transcendent. This description has four essential elements: first, religion is systematic; second, it is practical; third, it is an attempt to find meaning; and fourth, it appeals to the transcendent. Let me say something briefly about these four ideas, whose exposition will be the substance of the rest of the book.

First, the systematic. Being genuinely religious is not simply having a vague sense of the spiritual, significant as this psychological phenomenon may be. Rather, it essentially involves a collection of ideas and practices that are designed to fit together. Someone does not count as religious simply because they think there is more to the world than what we see around us every day; this belief has to be fitted into a system of beliefs or metaphors or stories—about God and the sacred, for example, and about how to live one's life from day to day. This system of thought and other attitudes are often embodied in sacred texts and developed in the official doctrines or the theology of a religious group. I mention here other attitudes, metaphors, and stories to accommodate the fact that many believers do not take themselves to hold doctrines that allow of strict literal expression as beliefs. More on this later.

Second, religion is practical. It involves not just believing in certain propositions or doctrines, or knowing certain stories, but also it involves acting in a certain way. Two broad kinds of action are important: the first is the participation in religious rituals, either collectively or individually; and the second is the group of actions directed at other people, such as codes of behavior and practices of morality or charity. This illustrates how morality is part of the practical element of religion, but it is not the whole of it— something I will return to in Chapter 3.

Third, meaning. It is of course a familiar idea that religion is a search for life's meaning. But not every search for meaning is religious. Some people find meaning in their relationships with loved ones, their children, and their families. Others find it in their experience of art, music, and beautiful things; others in developing their life plans, or in their ethical, moral, or political lives. But this does not touch the question of the meaning *of our lives as a whole*. James Tartaglia has pointed out that when philosophers answer that question by talking about the meaning *in* a person's life, they have in effect changed the subject, often without acknowledging it.[7] Simon Blackburn, for example, briskly reminds those atheists who might find the world meaningless that "there is plenty of meaning to be found during life. The smile of a baby means the world to the mother; successes mean a lot to those who have struggled to achieve them, and so on."[8] These things, and the attempts I have just mentioned, are attempts to find meaning *in* life; religion, as I see it, attempts to find the meaning *of* life as a whole, what Armstrong has called the "investment of everything with ultimate meaning."[9]

Looking for the meaning of life is not the same as looking for an understanding of the world, of how things as a whole hang together. It is true that this kind of understanding—from science, or from metaphysics—can result in "making sense of things."[10] But this understanding is not the same as the religious grasp of the meaning of life. As Thomas Nagel says, "It is important to distinguish [the religious] question from the pure desire for understanding of the universe and one's place in it."[11] The religious question, according to Nagel, is, "How can one bring into one's individual life a full recognition of one's relation to the universe as a whole?"[12]

The religious answer to this question, stated most broadly and abstractly, is that one should live one's entire life in an awareness of the transcendent—this is the fourth idea in terms of which I am defining religion. The transcendent is something that is beyond this world: beyond the ordinary, the everyday, the world of experience, and the world of science too. Living in the awareness of the transcendent is the way to achieve meaning, according to the religious point of view. The religious search for meaning ends in the transcendent. John Cottingham has argued, for example, that the religious life involves responding to "intimations of a transcendent world of meaning that breaks through into the ordinary world of our five senses."[13]

It is common, as we shall see, to describe the religious commitment to the transcendent as a commitment to the "supernatural" and to "supernatural entities." To my mind, this is a somewhat problematic description in a number of ways. For one thing, belief in the supernatural cannot be sufficient for religious belief since it will not distinguish religion from magic (which, as Durkheim showed, is crucial for gaining a correct conception of religion). Second, the appeal to the idea of the supernatural relies on a conception of nature according to which nature, an autonomous, law-governed whole, is opposed to God and the divine. This conception of nature is a product of the scientific revolution of the seventeenth century, and it would surely not have been acknowledged before that time. Durkheim, writing in 1912, put it well:

The idea of the supernatural is of recent vintage: it presupposes its opposite, which it negates and which is not at all primitive. In order to call certain phenomena supernatural, one must already have the sense that there is a natural order of things, in other words that the phenomena of the universe are connected to one another according to certain necessary relationships called laws.[14]

So if we want to describe what I call the religious impulse from the point of view of the tradition in which it belongs, then we should not build the idea of the supernatural into our definition of religion. This why I define it in terms of the transcendent rather than the supernatural.

The transcendent is something beyond or outside our experience. Religion is the systematic, practical attempt to align oneself with the transcendent, and God (under various names and guises) is the principal way in which the transcendent has been conceived. But to get a proper overview of religion as a phenomenon, we should not start by just introducing God as a hypothesized entity and building our whole conception of religious belief outward from there. Rather, we should understand claims about God in the context of all the other elements of religion—in particular, the two central aspects I will describe in more detail in Chapters 2 and 3: what I call the "religious impulse" and "identification." The religious impulse is the need to live one's life in harmony with the transcendent (for example, the will of God). And "identification" is my term for the fact that religions are social institutions; the fact that, as Durkheim says, one does not just believe in a religion, one belongs to it.

My rough definition of religion is therefore somewhat different from the definitions given by some recent atheist writers. Daniel C. Dennett defines religions as "social systems whose participants avow belief in a supernatural agent or agents whose approval is to be sought."[15] A. C. Grayling says that "by definition a religion is something centred upon belief in the existence of supernatural agencies or entities in the universe."[16] And Richard Dawkins describes what he calls the "God Hypothesis," that "there exists a superhuman, supernatural intelligence who deliberately designed and created the universe and everything in it, including us."[17] What is common to these views is that religion is characterized principally in terms of supernatural agency. It is true that Dennett, Grayling, and Dawkins do not say that the belief in a supernatural agency is the whole of religious belief. But in making this idea so central to their conception, they give what I consider to be a distorted view of religious phenomena. The distortion comes with ignoring the element of practice and community (what I call identification) and conceiving of the metaphysical side of religious belief in terms that are at once too sophisticated and too simplistic—too sophisticated because religious believers need not operate with the clear-cut idea of the supernatural attributed to them by today's philosophers and scientists, and too simplistic because the idea of God is not simply the idea of a supernatural agent who made the world; this is the truth in the familiar charge that the New Atheists have a "fundamentalist" or "literalist" conception of religious belief. As the anthropologist Pascal Boyer observes,

If people tell you "Religion is faith in a doctrine that teaches us how to save our souls by obeying a wise and eternal creator of the universe," these people probably have not travelled or read widely enough.[18]

This would be a good place to emphasize that when I talk about the "more sophisticated" content of religious belief, I am not talking about what theologians or philosophers think. The views I discuss here and in Chapter 2 are not the complex philosophies or theologies developed by scholars over the centuries. Theology is one thing, religion is another. What I am trying to do is to give a description, from the outside, of the most general aspects of anything that counts as a religious worldview. But this worldview is the worldview of religious believers themselves—insofar as it is possible to generalize the views of billions of people. Again, this may strike you as an impossible or absurd ambition, but we have no choice but to attempt to do this if we let ourselves generalize about "religion" at all.

The important point is this: to understand a philosophy or a worldview, it is not enough simply to list the propositions held by some or all of those who subscribe to it. One also must understand what is central to the view and what is peripheral. The descriptions given by Dennett and others place the single idea of a supernatural agency at the center of the religious worldview. In the next two chapters I will describe a different kind of center.

Having given my initial characterization of religion, let me say a little about belief itself. Philosophers use the word "belief" to refer to any commitment to the truth of some proposition or claim. So in this sense of the word, any opinion whatsoever—however weighty or trivial—counts as a belief. Your views about life after death, about the next U.S. president, about the price of milk, about tomorrow's weather—these all count as "beliefs" in philosophical discussions.

What is it to believe something in this sense? Belief is a psychological state, a state of mind; but it is not a conscious state of mind, since no one is ever conscious of all the things that they believe at one given moment. It's rather that when a conscious human being believes something, they are capable of bringing what they believe to consciousness, reflecting on it, and considering it in the light of other things they believe. If someone asks you, for example, what the weather will be like tomorrow, then you can reflect on what you believe about this, and you can answer (even if the answer is "no idea"). This is not so with other properties or attributes you have. Take your weight, for example: you cannot know what you weigh right now simply by reflecting on it. The other psychological feature of belief is that our beliefs govern our actions. What we do depends partly on what we believe and partly on what we want. So if someone believes that the weather will be cold tomorrow, and they don't want to get too cold, they will act appropriately: staying indoors, dressing in warm clothes, and so on.

It is a truism that for every belief, there must be something that is believed. It is not possible to have a belief without believing anything. What is believed is known as the "content" of the belief. So the content of the belief that the weather will be cold tomorrow is simply that *the weather will be cold tomorrow.* Beliefs are distinguished from one another by their different contents. It is similarly a truism that the content of a belief can be true or false: it's true if it will be cold tomorrow, false if not.

When we talk about the truth or falsity of a belief, then, we are really talking about whether the content of the belief is true or false. Applied to our simple example, the belief that it will be cold tomorrow is true when its content is true: when it is true that it will be cold tomorrow. And the belief is false when its content is false. Some beliefs are true (correct) and some false (incorrect), but this fact is independent of whether they are believed. Believing something is *taking* it to be true, and this is what matters to the believer. One cannot simultaneously believe something and be neutral on whether it is true—there is something paradoxical about saying, "I believe that it will rain but I have no opinion on whether it is true that it will rain." Philosophers sometimes express this by saying that belief *aims at truth*.

On the standard philosophical conception, then, belief involves these elements: accessibility to consciousness, a connection to action, and the aim toward truth. Outside philosophy, however, the word "belief" often refers only to opinions about important matters. If you said, outside a philosophical discussion, "I firmly believe that I am now wearing socks," people would probably make their excuses and leave. Beliefs in the ordinary sense are supposed to be about something important or valuable, something meaningful that governs your whole life or being—politics, ethics, identity, or religion—hence the title of this book.

However, the standard philosophical account of belief is perfectly compatible with this fact. Beliefs in the everyday sense are beliefs whose contents concern important matters about your whole life; but what makes a belief a *belief* is the same in every case. In particular, the features that philosophers identify as essential to belief—accessibility to consciousness, the connection to action, and the aim at truth—all apply equally to religious belief. The religious can bring their belief to consciousness, their beliefs guide their actions in complex ways, and it is incoherent to suppose that someone has a religious belief and yet has no view on whether the content of that belief is true.

So philosophers are not talking about something different when they talk about belief; it's just that the examples they use are rather simple, banal ones. Their reason for doing this is so they don't distract from the main theme they are discussing, which is belief itself, belief as such—rather than being sidetracked into discussing the interesting features of the world that some beliefs are about.

My aim here is different. I do not have anything new to say here about the mental state of belief as such. My interest is in the content of religious belief. The first thing we need to address, then, is belief in God, and its opposite, atheism. I will say more about the content of religious belief in Chapter 2.

ATHEISM

Atheism may be quite simply defined as disbelief in God, or the denial of God's existence. As characterized by the different monotheistic faiths, God is a transcendent being, not simply another entity in the ordinary, mundane world. So to deny the transcendent entails denying God. My own atheism is a consequence of my denial of the transcendent. I believe the world around us that we experience, together with the invisible world described by science, is all there is. Nothing transcends it. It follows from this that

I also must believe God does not exist. (Remember that I am discussing the meaning, not the truth, of religious belief; so I'm not going to defend the atheist position here. I'm just describing it.)

It is possible, of course, to maintain a belief in the transcendent and deny God in any of the ways conceived by traditional monotheistic religious doctrines. Some forms of mysticism are like this. Durkheim pointed out long ago that "there are great religions in which the idea of gods and spirits are absent," and anthropologists today agree.[19] The conception of religion I sketch in this book does, I think, apply to religions without one single deity like Buddhism and Hinduism. But my focus here will be on the monotheistic religions I know most about; hence my interest in atheism.

Atheism—the claim that God does not exist—is an idea that is sometimes misunderstood, and sometimes represented as being something it is not. It is often distinguished from agnosticism, the view that in our current state of knowledge we are not in a position to say whether God exists. Atheism is a more committed position: it says we are in such a position, and we should answer in the negative. Sometimes atheism is described as an "arrogant" view, presumably because atheists see the question of God's existence as settled. But there is nothing arrogant about treating an issue as settled if you have taken into account all the relevant knowledge, arguments, and evidence to the best of your ability. Arrogance is better thought of as a quality of what you do with your belief when you have settled on it—how you act, how you express your belief, how you treat others who disagree, and so on—rather than a quality of the belief itself.

Atheism and agnosticism are genuinely distinct positions. Neither of them, however, offers any positive substantial doctrines about what the world is like or how we should live. Some people are bothered by this: by the fact that atheism, so described, is a negative position. A significant collection of essays by atheist philosophers is advertised as recommending atheism as a "profoundly fulfilling and moral way of life," as a contrast to those who think of it as a negative outlook on life.[20] In his short introduction to atheism, Julian Baggini considers the view that atheism is just "parasitic on religion and by its very nature negative" but rightly concludes that this view involves a fallacy, the result of drawing too much out of the etymology of the word "atheism."[21] He goes on to propose a "positive" version of atheism. But I cannot see the objection to negative views as such; if I am against imprisonment without trial and torture, then my belief is negative in the above sense. It is parasitic on the existence of torture and imprisonment without trial. And even if torture were wiped out, this fact would be "parasitic" on the previous existence of torture. How can this be an objection to my belief?

Atheism does have *some* positive content, however, in the sense that it is an explicit acknowledgment of the factuality of some central religious beliefs: the idea that in some way or another, religious belief is answerable to something in the world, that it must ultimately be assessed in terms of how things actually are, of what really happened. This is perhaps most explicit in Christianity. The theologian David Bentley Hart states that "Christianity is the only major faith built entirely around a single historical claim."[22] Saint Paul was explicit: "If Christ be not risen, then is our preaching vain, and your faith is also vain."[23] Christian belief is committed to the factuality of certain real events: the crucifixion, the resurrection, and so on, whatever these events may have exactly involved; and to the reality of the transcendent, mysterious as it may be. Atheism acknowledges this, and so its positive content is that reality is different from the way Christianity (for example) says it is.

Apart from its rejection of God, then, what further attitudes do atheists take toward the phenomenon of religious belief? Some atheist movements adopt the relentlessly combative approach to religion promoted by the New Atheists—Dawkins, Dennett, Grayling, Sam Harris, and Christopher Hitchens. As these writers present things, religion contains little of value: it is irrational, its doctrines verge on the nonsensical, and it is the cause of many of the world's major problems.

It is worth noting, though, that not all recent atheist writers take this hostile approach. Some thinkers who reject existing organized religion or specific theological doctrine nonetheless see value in aspects of religion. Ronald Dworkin, in his *Religion without God,* argues that the essence of religion is the view that "inherent, objective value permeates everything," and this is independent of belief in God or the transcendent.[24] Alain de Botton has argued in a different way for a "religion for atheists" in which the insights of Christianity can be gleaned to help us with the "challenges of community and of mental and bodily suffering" by providing new rituals and ways of being together.[25]

Given the way I am conceiving religion, these philosophers are not really proposing an "atheist religion" at all. Religion without transcendence is no religion, and I will explain why in Chapter 2. I share these thinkers' opposition to the New Atheists. But I don't think an atheist can find genuine solace in religion. There are things to admire in the religious traditions in the world, but it is one thing to admire aspects of a religion and another to try to adopt its practices without believing its doctrines. What these "religious atheists" tend to lack are the two essential elements of religious belief I mentioned previously: what I call the religious impulse, and the element of identification. The religious impulse, roughly speaking, is the belief in the transcendent: "something beyond all this." The element of identification consists in the fact that religion involves institutions to which believers belong and practices in which they participate. Dworkin's *Religion without God* includes none of this. De Botton's *Religion for Atheists* does attempt to introduce a kind of identification, but it has no place for the religious impulse.

We could, I suppose, use the word "religion" for any belief system at all, thus making socialism, communism, environmentalism, scientism, humanism, secularism, and atheism all "religions" by stipulation. But what would be the point of this? If we decided to broaden the use of the word in this way, we would still need a word for those belief systems that affirm the reality of the transcendent and require certain rituals to be performed by believers in their expression of this commitment. It is far better to use the term "religion"—as it has been traditionally used—for these kinds of belief systems than it is to extend the word in this stipulative and misleading way. Nothing is gained by redefining words in debates like this; if you try to define a genuine, real phenomenon out of existence, it will only assert itself elsewhere.

HUMANISM

It should be uncontroversial, I think, that the content of atheism is determined by religion, since what it is denying is a central thesis of many of them: that a transcendent deity exists. In this sense, then, atheism is "parasitic" on religion. I don't see how (or why) it should be otherwise.

Yet some thinkers still seem to expect more from atheism, something in addition to its mere denial of God. This may be one of the motivations behind contemporary humanism, an active atheist movement in the United Kingdom, the United States, and elsewhere. Dawkins has called humanism "the ethical system that often goes with atheism" thus noting one distinction between the two views.[26] Humanists are those atheists who feel the need for a distinctive moral outlook and more—perhaps rituals, meetings, or a sense of community. Contemporary humanism was formed in reaction to religious belief, to give atheists something of a value system and system of practices to replace the religious values and practices. So, for example, there are now humanist child-naming ceremonies, funerals, and wedding rituals. Humanists want to create structures of belief, ritual, and practice that play a similar role to religious rituals.

The first "humanist manifesto," published in the United States in 1933, talked of humanism as a "new religion."[27] Nowhere does this ring more true than at weekend meetings of ethical societies in chilly and austere halls that can resemble Methodist chapels or downbeat versions of Christian Science temples. Some humanist groups in Britain were actually started as "Ethical Societies" by nonconformist Christians in the nineteenth century.[28] It is undeniable that a lot of what has passed for atheistical humanism can look from the outside like a kind of liberal nonconformism without the hymns. And just as Christianity has its saints' days, so some prominent humanists in the United States and the United Kingdom (including Dennett, Dawkins, and the British biologist Stephen Rose) have campaigned for a national holiday on Charles Darwin's birthday. Critics of humanism have sometimes tried to argue that these things support the view that humanism is a kind of religion itself. John Gray, for example, claims that "contemporary humanism is a religion that lacks the insight into human frailty of traditional faiths."[29]

But it is quite wrong to say that humanism is itself a religion. Not every social movement—not even those that have meetings on Sundays—is a religion, and not every moral code is a religious code. As I observed previously, unless we are going to stretch the meaning of the word beyond all usefulness, we should insist that a religion involves a commitment to the transcendent, which in the case of Western monotheism means belief in God. Without the transcendent, there is no religion. What this actually involves will be dealt with in a little more detail in Chapter 2.

It is a significant fact, though, that many atheists feel the need to belong to a movement, and that they feel the need for rituals to mark the important moments in life: birth, marriage, and death. For many atheists, the absence of religion leaves gaps that have to be filled by something else, and the creation of a movement can become the focus of this need. A striking and (to my mind) bizarre example of this is the Brights movement, founded in 2003 in the United States by a group of people who disliked the negative connotations of words like "atheist" and "godless." There are currently over fifty-eight thousand Brights in more than two hundred countries across the world, organized into local "constituencies," and the movement has been endorsed by Dawkins and Dennett, among other distinguished figures. In 2003 Dawkins compared the term "Bright" to the introduction of the word "gay" as a positive term for being homosexual:

Gay is succinct, uplifting, positive: an "up" word, where homosexual is a down word, and queer, faggot and pooftah are insults. Those of us who subscribe to no religion; those of us whose view of the universe is natural rather than supernatural; those of us who rejoice in the real and scorn the false comfort of the unreal, we need a word of our own, a word like "gay."[30]

The human need to belong is very important, and I will examine it further in Chapter 3. But despite the endorsement of Dawkins and others, it is clearly not an essential part of being a humanist that they belong to "ethical societies" or constituencies of Brights. It's not even necessary that all humanists believe in all of the same things. The humanist philosopher Richard Norman writes that "there is no humanist creed, no set of beliefs to which every humanist has to subscribe. Humanism is not a dogma or a sect."[31]

This of course raises the question of what humanism essentially is, and whether atheists are obliged to think of themselves as humanists. (Since I count myself as an atheist who is not a humanist, I'm taking it for granted that atheism is not the same thing as humanism.) "Humanism" has meant a number of things over the centuries. The humanism of the Italian Renaissance, which flourished from the fourteenth to the sixteenth centuries, was a philosophy that rejected the dominance of the dry and remote theories of the "schools"—the medieval universities of Paris, Padua, Rome, Oxford, and so on—and promoted the rediscovery of the "human." Contemporary humanism has little to do with this Renaissance tradition, not least because Renaissance humanism was not atheistic. Contemporary atheistic humanism in England has a distinguished history too, stemming back to the nineteenth century, when its pioneers shared many of the progressive social ideas of religious social reformers. These humanist movements have many connections with the liberal ideals of British writers such as John Stuart Mill and Jeremy Bentham.

Unsurprisingly for a doctrine called "humanism," the atheist humanist tradition places great emphasis on the importance of the human. As the International Ethical and Humanist Union states in one of its bylaws:

Humanism is a democratic and ethical life stance, which affirms that human beings have the right and responsibility to give meaning and shape to their own lives. It stands for the building of a more humane society through an ethic based on human and other natural values in the spirit of reason and free inquiry through human capabilities. It is not theistic, and it does not accept supernatural views of reality.[32]

A similar emphasis on the importance of the human is given by Norman:

We possess distinctively human capacities for rational thought and action, and we should use them as best we can, along with our equally human capacities for love and care and compassion, to resist the cruelty and the inhumanity which led to the concentration camps.[33]

Norman appeals to the use of distinctively human capacities as the remedy for the ills of civilization, and many humanists pursue the idea that the human is, in some way, the ultimate source of value in the world. This is an appealing (though controversial) idea, and clearly one worth taking seriously. But should atheists adopt it?

Gray pours scorn on those who talk about the value of distinctively human capacities: "When the claim that humans are radically different from other animals is wrenched from its theological roots it is not just indefensible but virtually incomprehensible."[34] But this is really very hard to believe: there are many true and important things one can say about the distinctive nature of human beings that have nothing to do with the theological roots of this idea. A group of leading ethologists puts it nicely:

Human animals—and no other—build fires and wheels, diagnose each other's illnesses, communicate using symbols, navigate with maps, risk their lives for ideals, collaborate with each other, explain the world in terms of hypothetical causes, punish strangers for breaking rules, imagine impossible scenarios, and teach each other how to do all of the above.[35]

Given these obvious facts, it is pointless to insist that nothing is distinctively human, simply because some (more or less) similar things are also done by nonhuman animals.

One of the things that human beings do is attach value to things, of course—to actions, practices, rituals, and objects. But this fact does not imply that the human is the only *source* of value, even if we have rejected the transcendent as a source of value. There may be sources of value other than God or the human. Consider, for example, the utilitarianism invented by Mill and

Bentham: the doctrine that the foundation of morality is "the greatest happiness of the greatest number." If we understand happiness (as some utilitarians did) in essentially sensory terms (in terms of sensory pleasure and the absence of pain), then the quantity of happiness in the world is not limited by the quantity of human happiness; there is plenty of animal pleasure and pain to take into account. And as utilitarians like Peter Singer have argued, if we think of the basis of morality in this way, then it is objectionable prejudice to treat nonhuman animals (those capable of feeling pain) differently from humans. This of course was Bentham's view: the question about animals, he famously argued, was not "can they reason? nor, can they talk? but, can they suffer?"[36]

Another way one might reject the idea of the human as the source of all value is via Dworkin's idea, mentioned previously, that an "inherent, objective value permeates everything." This way of thinking would reject the idea that value can only derive from the human, since Dworkin's idea of objective value is not the idea of human-derived value. Yet another, more extreme, way to reject the idea of all value derived from the human is to deny that there is any value at all. This nihilist view of the world is doubtless unattractive, but it is compatible with atheism and therefore illustrates my general point: that atheism as such does not require the idea that all value derives from the human.

The view that humanity is the source of all value is an interesting one, well worth discussing. But it is not required by atheism—the rejection of a transcendent deity—so if this is what humanism is, atheists need not be humanists. Atheism, a mere factual, negative thesis, entails no specific view about the nature of morality. Humanism, insofar as it elevates the human as the source of all morality, is a further thesis.

So I will not address specific humanist claims in the rest of this book. Instead I will attempt to enter the debate between New Atheists and believers. It will be obvious to all readers that apart from its bad temper, the most striking feature of this debate is its stagnation. The New Atheists pile argument upon argument against religion, and the religious are as unmoved by them as the New Atheists are unmoved by any part of the defense of religion. We don't really have a debate at all, in fact; just people talking past each other or shouting at each other.

The fact that so many highly intelligent educated people can make no impact on one another in their arguments ought to give us pause for thought. Why is it that the atheist arguments—many of which are plausible and some unanswerable—have made almost no impact on religious believers? Why do the New Atheists rarely engage with religious thinkers and their views directly? And why do the more articulate religious thinkers who engage with the New Atheists charge them with simply missing the point?

In the rest of this book I will answer these questions. Many objections have been made to the New Atheists: that they are "shrill," disrespectful, aggressive, or even quasi-religious or "fundamentalist" themselves. There may be some truth in some (or all) of these charges; but none of them is my objection to the New Atheists. My principal objection is that they have an inadequate conception of religion, and this is largely why they are ignored by those they criticize: most religious believers simply do not recognize themselves in the picture of religion painted by the New Atheists. This is why there is no debate: if you want a genuine debate about religion, you need to give an accurate account of the phenomenon itself. In Chapters 2 and 3 I will attempt to sketch such an account.

2

The Religious Impulse

THE UNSEEN ORDER

According to William James, "Were one asked to characterise the life of religion in the broadest and most general terms, one might say that it consists in the belief that there is an unseen order, and that our supreme good lies in harmoniously adjusting ourselves thereto."[1] This belief is what I will call the religious impulse. One central theme of this book is that James is partly right: the religious impulse is one of the *two* essential components of religious belief. I will discuss this component in the current chapter. The other essential component—what

I call the element of identification—will be discussed in Chapter 3.

James's remark contains two ideas: first, that there is an unseen order, and, second, that the good consists in living in accord with it. The idea of an unseen order is not simply the idea that reality extends beyond the visible; this should be accepted by everyone. Science postulates invisible structures—atoms, electrons, quarks, forces, and so on—to explain visible phenomena. These things are unseen, and in some sense they form an order too, the order determined by the laws of nature, whatever these turn out to be.

The unseen order James talks about is something else. The order physics talks about is order as contrasted with randomness or chaos; but the order that is the focus of the religious impulse is a normative order, the order of how things *ought* to be. Order in the natural world is a matter of things behaving in a regular way: dropped objects fall to the ground because of gravity, sodium explodes in water because the interaction produces hydrogen that ignites, a peeled apple turns brown because of an enzyme that oxidizes. The other kind of order is not about things behaving in a regular way but about things behaving in the way they should (it's order as in "law and order," so to speak).

The distinction between how things generally are and how they should be is the distinction between what is "normal" and what is "normative." Normality and normativity are very different concepts. Normality is just a matter of regularity, whereas normativity is a matter of conforming to some kind of standard or ideal. So, for example, the normativity of morality is a matter of conforming to a moral ideal—the ideal of doing the right thing. The normativity of rationality is a matter of conforming to an intellectual ideal—the ideal of being reasonable. Falling objects do not conform to Newton's inverse square law of universal gravitation in this sense; the law is a description of what normally happens, not a prescription of what ought to happen.

What normative ideal is implicated in the religious impulse? What is the "religious ideal," as we might call it? This is probably the most difficult abstract question, when applied to specific religions. In its vaguest outline, though, the answer should be clear to all who have thought hard about the nature of religion: the religious ideal is to live life according to God's will, or the will of Allah, or in accord with the prescriptions of the laws that embody these divine wills. The harmony that James talks about is what Christians talk about when they talk about living in harmony with the will of God. It is the harmony that comes when one lives in accord with how things ought to be. The difficulty lies in saying in detail what this exactly means.

A widespread expression of the religious impulse is the familiar thought that *this can't be all there is; there must be something more to the world.* What lies behind this thought? It is not the idea that we don't know what the world is like in its entirety. It is not an expression of frustration at our ignorance. Nor is it just the feeling that it would be better if there were more to the world (more time, more space, more galaxies . . .) than there actually is. Simon Blackburn attributes to the believer the view that what they desire is more of the same, more of *this:*

I am sorry for people who cannot find any meaning or purpose in their lives, but I certainly do not see that living on and on and on forever would cure that: if anything, it would seem to make things worse. Schopenhauer thought that boredom was only second to actual pain as an evil to be avoided. I find it very odd that people who can barely stand an hour of singing and praying and praising in church on Sunday can imagine being blissfully happy doing nothing else for eternity. They must have very poor imaginations.[2]

But the way I see things, this remark misses the point. The religious desire would not be satisfied if we were merely to live longer, or even forever, doing the same things as we do in our earthly lives (including worship and attending church). Perhaps someone might express some religious urge with these words, but this is not the familiar idea I am talking about. After all, no one really has any idea what it would be like to live forever in the same way as we do now; this is not something someone could coherently and literally wish for or desire. The familiar idea is rather that the mundane world we experience in everyday life, plus the world we find out about in science, must contain some kind of point or meaning, something that might not be detectable by all observers. Days follow one another, a generation comes and a generation goes. If this were all there is, then the world would be meaningless. The religious impulse involves the view that the world is not meaningless. Therefore, all this cannot be all there is.

Religion attempts to make sense of the world by seeing a kind of meaning or significance in things. This kind of significance does not need laws or generalizations, just the sense that the everyday world we experience is not all there is, and that behind it all is the mystery of God's presence, or, more abstractly, the unseen order. The believer is convinced that God is present in everything, and the divine presence makes sense of their life by suffusing it with meaning. This is the attitude expressed in George Herbert's poem "The Elixir": "Who sweeps a room as for Thy laws / Makes that and th' action fine."[3] Equipped with the religious impulse, even the most miserable tasks can come to have value.

The feeling of the meaninglessness of the world, which the religious impulse is set against, is one of the dominant ideas of the modern era. Max Weber called this the "disenchantment" of the world, and the term has stuck.[4] Some trace the origins of the idea of disenchantment to the Enlightenment, others trace it to Nicolaus Copernicus or to the rise of modern science in the seventeenth century, others see contributions made to it by the ideas of Charles Darwin, Marx, and Sigmund Freud. There are surely many different ideas here, and it's not my purpose to distinguish them, since what they all have in common is the rejection of the notion that there is an unseen order and that our highest good is achieved by living in accord with that order. The disenchanted vision of the world sees no order other than the order of the laws of nature. So it needs some other account of our highest good, if one can be found at all.

There are two popular atheist responses to the apparent disenchantment of the world. I will call them the pessimist's response and the optimist's response. The pessimist's response is to accept that the world is in and of itself thoroughly disenchanted but also to assert that we should try to make the best of it. The pessimist concedes that the religious believer is in a certain sense right: if God does not exist, or if there is no unseen order, the world is at bottom meaningless. For there is no ultimate purpose in what Philip Larkin called "all the uncaring, intricate, rented world," so any meaning there is must be something we have to create for ourselves.[5] But this meaning will never amount to "re-enchantment": in the terms introduced in Chapter 1, we can only find meaning *in* life, not the meaning *of* life.

The optimist's response is to question the idea that the world is really disenchanted, perhaps on the grounds that the idea that the world might be "enchanted" in the religious sense is actually a kind of myth or confusion, or an impossibility. According to the optimist, when we try to spell out what it really means for anything to be enchanted, we can see that our everyday lives can be as enchanted as anything that the religious can offer, and indeed they might even be enchanted in a genuinely more authentic sense. The optimist says that the believer's sense of enchantment is deeply confused; there can be no such thing. So it's best not to talk about enchantment at all. But this does not matter because whatever it is that the pessimist and the religious believer thought was good about enchantment can be obtained in the modern secular world.

Although the pessimist and the optimist may give the same kind of advice for those looking for enchantment—look for meaning in your relationships; fulfill yourself through your children, your projects, good works, charity, knowledge, art, and so on—they actually hold very different views. The pessimist fully acknowledges the ultimate meaninglessness and disenchantment of the world without an unseen order. But the optimist, by contrast, rejects the assumptions that give rise to disenchantment.

This is important because it is only really the pessimist who takes the religious impulse seriously. For in acknowledging that the world is disenchanted, they acknowledge that the idea of enchantment is intelligible: one cannot deny what does not make sense; one can only reject the whole way of talking that embodies this supposed nonsense. The pessimist says that what the religious people believe in isn't actually true of our world: our world is not enchanted, though in some sense it could have been. And if enchantment is intelligible, the religious impulse is too. The optimist, however, tends to dismiss the idea of enchantment as an incoherent fantasy—and with it, the religious impulse itself.

To illustrate this contrast, consider these two atheist approaches applied to the question of religion and morality. The pessimist concedes that if God existed, then morality would make sense in a way that it does not make sense now; but since God does not exist, we need to understand morality in a different way. The optimist argues that even if God existed, this would not make sense of morality—perhaps because morality cannot be justified in terms of submitting oneself to the command of some other being (for example). So on this approach, morality with God doesn't really make sense; the challenge in understanding morality is not about making sense of it in a world without God. It's about making sense of it *tout court*.

Another illustration is the case of Christian art. Many atheists are happy to admit that some of the indisputably greatest works of art are religious in content and in inspiration. After everything that has been written on this subject, it seems hardly necessary to list the usual examples (Bach's *St. Matthew Passion,* Michelangelo's frescoes in the Sistine Chapel, the magnificent cathedrals of Europe, and so on). One question about religious art is whether the value of the work of art, or the value of the experience it offers, would be greater if the religious vision that inspired it were true. Pessimist atheists say that it would. Optimist atheists say it wouldn't; indeed, optimists may argue that their experience of religious art shows how the meaning and significance of a work of art does not rely on the truth of extrinsic ideas; it can be, so to speak, thoroughly self-sufficient.

In general, the pessimist acknowledges that the world would have some significant meaning if God existed; but the optimist rejects even the *possibility* that God's existence could give the world meaning. All that meaning could be is the kind of meaning that a world without God has. Kenneth Taylor summarizes the optimist's view nicely when he says,

There is almost nothing to be said for either the view that belief in providence provides invincible armour against despair or for the view that the atheist who rejects providence need surrender to a paralyzing despair.[6]

Nonetheless, both the pessimistic and the optimistic responses see the religious impulse as a misrepresentation of the facts about the meaninglessness of the world. Larkin once described religion as "that vast moth-eaten musical brocade / Created to pretend we never die."[7] The suggestion that religion is a form of pretense or deception (of the self or otherwise) is also common among New Atheist writers: they charge the religious with not facing up to death or to the ultimate contingency of everything. Pessimists may say that they are just making a mistake about the extent of reality, or that their religion involves a lack of knowledge or vision;

optimists are more likely to say it involves some kind of deep confusion.

I am a pessimistic atheist. I think the religious impulse is intelligible, but I agree with Thomas Nagel when he says that "the universe revealed by chemistry and physics, however beautiful and awe-inspiring, is meaningless, in the strict sense that it is wholly lacking in meaning."[8] Weber himself was slightly more cautious: "It is simply not self-evident that something which is subject to [scientific] law is in itself meaningful."[9] So I do not think it is a confusion to see a meaningful life in terms of aligning oneself with the unseen order; nor do I think it need involve some kind of deep self-deception. Rather, I think it is clearly an intelligible human reaction to the mystery of the world, one that has dominated much of what has ever counted as human society.

Some will agree that the religious impulse, or something like it, is a pervasive feature of human beings, and that this is because it derives from part of human psychology, something that can be investigated scientifically. Some cognitive scientists treat religious belief as a natural upshot of the functioning of the human cognitive system. They sometimes use the term "counterintuitive beliefs" to characterize the specifically religious outputs of the human belief system.[10]

To think of religious belief as involving the possession of counterintuitive beliefs is a simplification in at least two respects. First, insofar as these counterintuitive beliefs are supposed to be beliefs in supernatural agencies, the approach identifies religious belief with belief about theoretical matters. As I explained in Chapter 1, belief in the philosophical sense is simply the idea of the commitment to the truth of any proposition. One can believe in this sense that there are apples in the basket, that it will rain tomorrow, that your children love you, or that Armageddon is imminent. Belief is the same whatever its content. But the more complex the content, the more it has the consequence of engaging the emotions and playing a central role in governing action, attitudes, and life plans. I think that religious belief has this more complex content. The belief in the truth of the ("counterintuitive") proposition that there exists a supernatural agency beyond the world of experience need not, on its own, have these consequences.

The second way in which the idea of counterintuitive beliefs is a simplification is that it assumes a standard of what is "intuitive" that derives from the beliefs of contemporary scientific, secular culture. These beliefs seem perfectly reasonable, and therefore intuitive, to people like me. But to figure out whether someone else's belief is intuitive requires that we immerse ourselves in their world and see what is central to their worldview and what is peripheral. From the Western scientific point of view, the idea that life as a whole, or the universe, might have some kind of point or purpose might strike us as counterintuitive. But, of course, this is partly because the scientific point of view started life as a rejection of this idea, with the rejection of Aristotelian teleology (goal-directedness) and the development of the purely mechanical view of the universe. Those starting from other places will find other views counterintuitive.

This is not relativism about truth—the modern Western scientific view is unquestionably superior to the Aristotelian view in its claims to describe the world, of course. The point is about what it means to say something is *intuitive* or *obvious* or *natural* to believe. What people find natural depends on the specific circumstances of their upbringing, their culture, and their level of knowledge. What needs to be addressed when looking at religion as a psychological or social phenomenon is not what seems "counterintuitive" to the contemporary scientific mind but how the participants themselves regard their own religious belief. This is not going to be the whole story, of course, since the nature of religion is a larger thing than what any specific collection of believers thinks it is. But to try to understand a human practice from the point of view of the practitioners should be the anthropological starting point.

For these reasons I am skeptical about some claims made by the cognitive science of religion. But does this mean that there is no distinctive psychological attitude that lies behind the religious impulse? James thought there is not:

One man allies it to the feeling of dependence; one makes it a derivative from fear; others connect it with the sexual life; others still identify it with the feeling of the infinite; and so on. Such different ways of conceiving it ought of themselves to arouse doubt as to whether it can possibly be one specific thing . . . nothing whatever of a psychologically specific nature.[11]

Others disagree. Nagel has described the aspiration "to live not merely the life of the creature one is, but in some sense to participate through it in the life of the universe as a whole," and he calls the need to have this aspiration or desire the "religious temperament."[12] The word "temperament" suggests a disposition of character or a character trait: not simply a belief but something more complex involving hope or aspiration and an emotional alignment to the world.

One way to interpret Nagel's idea of a religious temperament is in terms of the human tendency to see the world as suffused with meaning. Seeing meaning in everything is not just a matter of belief in the truth of some proposition. It involves belief, to be sure; but it also involves something that is more analogous to perception, or an emotional coloring of the world. Not all ways of apprehending the world cognitively are beliefs. When you walk into a room and you sense a tension among people you know, this is an immediate emotional recognition of something that is more akin to perception than to belief. More visceral yet is the awareness of fear; in the presence of something frightening, our bodies respond in ways that are automatic but may nonetheless be rational.

The complexity of our individual psychologies and the vastness of humanity are such that there will be no simple correlation between those who have a religious temperament and those who identify as religious. Some people have the urge to believe, to look for an unseen order, even if they are not actually believers. Some of the pessimistic atheists described previously are surely like this. In a sense, these people have a religious temperament, or the potential for it. There are those who would like to believe but cannot; those who look for order even though they also suspect that there is none. It is common for such people to describe themselves as spiritual, or as "searching" for something else. In the way I am thinking of things, these people may have something like a religious temperament without actually being believers.

Conversely, there are those who belong to religious faiths but who lack a religious temperament. For example, there are those who think of their membership of a religious group purely in what we might call "worldly" terms. Such people go to church, synagogue, or mosque, and they perform the religious observances required by their faith, but they have no belief in an unseen order and do not conceive of their moral life in terms of living in harmony with it. Nonetheless, it would be wrong to say such people are not "religious" in any sense at all, since they may be fully absorbed into the religious life on a practical, day-to-day basis, and their morality may well be deeply based on the traditions embodied in their religious texts. But it is perfectly intelligible to suppose that such people lack a religious temperament in Nagel's sense.

In my experience, many Christians and Jews live like this. Many Jews observe the rituals involved in keeping kosher, observing the Sabbath, and praying at the synagogue. It is of supreme importance in their lives that they are Jews, that what they are doing is what their parents and grandparents did, and that their lives would not make any real sense without it. But this does not mean that they are driven by the idea of a hidden order, something transcending ordinary experience with which they have to live in harmony. Some of these Jews, like some Christians (for example, nontheist Quakers or some liberal Anglicans in Britain) may well count as atheists, although they may not describe themselves in this way. But even if they don't actually declare themselves to be atheists, they may still lack a religious temperament.

We should distinguish then between what Nagel calls the religious temperament and what I call the religious impulse. The religious temperament a collection of different psychological traits; the religious impulse is the complex content of a specific belief. Since the belief that there is an unseen order is a part of the content of the religious impulse, the religious impulse is incompatible with atheism. Nonetheless, there are atheists who have many of the psychological traits associated with what Nagel calls the religious temperament.

The religious impulse is something that is central to religion as a phenomenon, but the religious temperament—a psychological attribute—may be unevenly spread among the practitioners of a faith. The next question is how much we can say, at this level of generality and abstraction, about the cognitive content of the religious impulse.

THE TRANSCENDENT
AND THE COSMOLOGICAL

The description I have given of the religious impulse will, I hope, be familiar to those who have studied the phenomenon of religious belief. If the religious impulse involves a belief, it must have a content—as I explained in Chapter 1, the content of a belief is what is believed, and it is not possible for someone to have a belief without them believing something. The content of the religious impulse is expressed in James's claim that there is an unseen order and that our greatest good is to live in harmony with this order. Different religions will work out what this means in their own way. But to state the obvious, this belief is a belief in the existence of something, and therefore a claim about the universe or the world as a whole—a cosmological claim.

While I reject the New Atheists' specific conception of religious cosmology, I want to insist that nonetheless there is this cosmological element in (most) religion. It has become popular for some atheists and Christians to play down this aspect of religious belief. But without the cosmological aspect, religious belief in the proper sense would not exist. For one can hardly aim to live one's life with the goal of being guided by the unseen order if there really is no such thing.

As we saw, James's talk of the "unseen order" is not about invisible aspects of reality: science has plenty of those. Rather, as I indicated in my basic characterization of religion in Chapter 1, it is about the *transcendent*. Philosophy and theology have traditionally contrasted the transcendent with the *immanent* (from the Latin *manere*, "to remain"). What is immanent is what "remains" within the world as we experience it; the transcendent goes beyond or surpasses this. The expression of the religious impulse that I mentioned previously, that "this can't be all there is," is an expression of belief in the transcendent. Sometimes people talk of the transcendent as being something other than "the world" or "this world"; or they might say that the world as a whole contains more than what is encountered in experience and science. These are really two ways of saying the same thing.

While some varieties of Christianity and Judaism have abandoned the ambition to talk about the transcendent, and see themselves as purely moral or ethical movements, I regard these varieties as peripheral to these great traditions. The appeal to the transcendent is an essential part of religion as I am conceiving it. There can be moral codes, practices, rituals, and the like—but I repeat my claim that without belief in something transcendent, there is no religion.

However, the mere idea that there is something cosmologically transcendent leaves it open what its nature actually is. The transcendent is, by definition, something *beyond:* beyond all this, everything we experience, everything we claim to fully understand. The various religions have understood the transcendent in different ways, but I think a common element in all of them is the idea that God or the divine (or whatever transcends) is not entirely intelligible to us. It is absolutely crucial to emphasize that this is not supposed to be a shortcoming of our belief; it's not as if, say, were we more intelligent or better informed, we would able to figure God out. The idea that God—or whatever transcends all *this*—is ultimately beyond our finite human understanding is something that is central to all religious traditions. John Gray has said that the "sense of mystery, the insight that the nature of things is finally unknowable" is central to Western monotheism.[13] He could have said it is central to all religion.

One consequence of the idea that we don't have a full cognitive grasp or understanding of the nature of the transcendent is that our attempts to know it often encounter obstacles when we try to express them fully or literally in words or images. This idea emerges in various places in the monotheistic religions: the idea that

the name of God (rendered "YHWH" in trans-
literation) cannot be uttered by devout Jews; the
idea that Muhammad must not be depicted at all;
and (more theologically) the medieval Christian
idea that God can only be describable in negative terms. This is not to say that orthodox versions of Judaism, Islam, and Christianity should
be regarded as mystical faiths, but only that they
place certain epistemic limits on believers: that
is, limits about what they can know.

The idea that the transcendent is something
that we, of necessity, cannot fully understand explains many things about religion. It explains
why believers are happy to utter day after day
words that they do not fully understand or that
involve metaphors and imagery that cannot be
rendered in literal terms without losing their
point. And it explains why rational, thoughtful
believers do not think that their view is refuted
when they are presented with what—from the
atheist's point of view—look like irrefutable
counterexamples.

For example, many atheists take the problem
of evil—how to reconcile the existence of pointless suffering and evil with the omnipotence
and goodness of God—to be something close to
a refutation of God's existence. One dominant

Christian response is that contrary to appearances, there must be some kind of underlying purpose in the suffering in the world, even if we cannot detect it. This response can prompt incomprehension or ridicule from the critics, and it can seem in some contexts almost improper, even in bad taste. How can one seriously say that there must be some underlying purpose to the appalling evil of the Holocaust? But some such response is, I claim, the correct one for those who attempt to live a life of faith. For these believers, we should not expect all aspects of the world to be intelligible—the idea that God moves in mysterious ways is not a "cop-out" but an unavoidable and troubling truth.

Not being a believer myself, I cannot properly enter into this way of thinking. But it is clearly something real in the minds of believers, and if we want to understand religion, we atheists have to try to appreciate it for what it is, however difficult it might be. I see this way of responding to the problem of evil as part of the acknowledgment of the mystery of God.

Looked at this way, the cosmological content of the religious impulse is quite different from Richard Dawkins's God Hypothesis described in Chapter 1: "There exists a superhuman, supernatural intelligence who deliberately designed and created the universe and everything in it, including us."[14] This is a straightforward, specific, factual claim about the nature of the unseen order that focuses on intelligence, design, and creation. Dawkins's idea differs from what I have identified as the religious impulse in at least three ways. First, it is certainly possible for someone to have the religious impulse and not believe that God is a "superhuman, supernatural intelligence." The unseen order need not involve any idea of something superhuman or any claim about intelligence. Second, the God Hypothesis says nothing about how to live, which is an essential part of the idea I took from James—our greatest good consists in living in harmony with this order. And third, Dawkins's hypothesis contains no suggestion that God might be beyond our understanding; yet, I claim, this too is an essential part of the religious traditions I am talking about.

Of course, the idea of creation by a supreme intelligence has been part of some religious narratives, but if we are going to have a more realistic and comprehensive picture of religious belief, we need to broaden our focus. In particular, we should reflect on the extent to which it is correct to talk of religious belief as a "hypothesis" at all.

When the great eighteenth-century physicist Pierre-Simon Laplace was asked about the place of God in his system of the universe, he is supposed to have replied, "I had no need of that hypothesis." Christopher Hitchens quotes Laplace approvingly but fails to acknowledge that Laplace's remark must have been intended to be provocative.[15] The idea that God might be a hypothesis along the lines of (say) Newton's hypothesis of universal gravitation would have struck Laplace's audience in a different way from the way it strikes Dawkins, Hitchens, or atheist readers these days. Laplace's remark was not made in an intellectual or social context in which God was just one hypothesis among others; indeed, talking of God as a hypothesis would probably have been considered grossly improper for a believer. So it would be simple-minded to take Laplace's remark simply as a scientific assessment of the God Hypothesis.

A hypothesis is a factual claim that is put forward as an attempt to explain some phenomena or data. One of Dawkins's points is that the God Hypothesis fares much worse in explaining things than his alternative evolutionary hypothesis, that "any creative intelligence, of sufficient complexity to design anything, comes into existence only as the end product of an extended process of gradual evolution."[16] There is no doubt that we should accept this latter hypothesis as a claim about our world; but the question is whether religious belief should be thought of as something comparable to this kind of hypothesis at all.

It's easy to see why one might say yes. A believer in divine creation will say in answer to the question, "where did the world come from?," that God created it. For a believer, this is a satisfactory explanation, but do they mean it as a good explanatory hypothesis in the scientific sense? The classic objection to it as a hypothesis, made by David Hume and repeated by many atheists since then, is that creation by God raises exactly the same questions as it answers. If the existence of the universe is explained by God's creative action, then what explains the existence of God?

In my experience, believers are typically not troubled by this question. If they were to take it seriously, then it ought to worry them. But although the question is often posed by skeptics and atheists, their opponents are not worried by it. Some critics might take this as yet another sign of the irrationality of believers: they postulate a creator to explain the world, and then they are unable to explain the creator—and what is worse, they are unworried by this! But there is another possible reading of this impasse: that the idea of God creating the world is not functioning as a hypothesis in the scientific sense at all. It's not as if God is just another object in the world that we hypothesize in order to explain the world—as we might hypothesize electrons to explain electromagnetic effects. For if that were the case, then it would be perfectly legitimate to ask what explains the existence of God (just as we can ask what explains the existence or nature of electrons). But for the believer, the appeal to God is not like the appeal to just another object: once we have reached God, that is all the explanation we need. God's existence does not need a further explanation.

A hypothesis should fit into a system of thought in which more complex or confusing things are explained in terms of simpler or clearer things. This scientific ideal is known as reduction: explanation that moves from the complex to the simpler. However, it's not obvious that the idea of God creating the world is in any intelligible sense simpler than the idea of the existence of the world. And rather than seeing this as a weakness of the religious explanation, I think we should see it as an indication that we are not in the realm of hypotheses, in the scientific sense, at all.

What religious claims contain that the very idea of a hypothesis does not is something that is arguably the most central aspect of religious cosmology: its claim to *meaning*. The religious impulse gives the believer's life meaning. It does this because it guides the believer in how to live life in accordance with the unseen order (or to live a life of piety, or faith, or holiness). When someone has faith, or the religious impulse, then it doesn't matter to them that there are certain questions they cannot answer. To ask the question, "If God made the world, then who made God?" just seems to miss the point for someone who actually is a believer, attempting to live a life in faith.

If religious claims are not hypotheses in the scientific sense, does this mean that they are not really claims about facts or existence at all? Dawkins will say yes, since he thinks that "religions make existence claims, and this means scientific claims."[17] So, for Dawkins, if something is not a scientific claim, then it cannot be an existence claim. But I am trying to put space between these two ideas. There are claims one can make about the world—and therefore about existence—that are not scientific.

Many examples from outside the sphere of religion illustrate this simple observation. Ordinary factual claims about human societies, like the fact that the European Union currently has twenty-eight members, or that the Second World War ended in 1945, are factual claims, or claims about existence—they make claims about what there is or was, or what happened and when. Yet there is no science of the European Union, and we did not need science to discover that the war ended in 1945. On the face of it, there are moral or political claims that also seem to be claims about existence, or factual claims about how things are—like the claim that there are forms of government that are superior to others (for example, democracy), or that there are things that are indisputably evil (for example, torture). And yet there is no science that will tell us which forms of government are superior, or what is good or evil. So on the face of it, factual or existence claims are not the same as scientific claims. Dawkins's equation of the two is incorrect.

Similarly, the idea that there is a transcendent order that extends beyond what we can experience is an existence claim that is not, I would say, scientific. Nor is the idea that our supreme good is to live in harmony with this order. The religious impulse is not a scientific hypothesis. Further reflection on this feature of religious belief will help us address the much-discussed question of whether science and religion are really compatible.

SCIENCE AND RELIGION

There is a story about Bertrand Russell giving a public lecture somewhere or other in which he defended his atheism. A furious woman stood up at the end of the lecture and asked, "And Lord Russell, what will you say when you stand in front of the throne of God on judgment day?" Russell replied, "I will say: I'm terribly sorry, but you didn't give us enough evidence."

This is a common way for atheists to react to religious claims: to ask for evidence, and often to reject these claims in its absence. In the context of the available evidence, the religious proto-scientific hypotheses do not seem to fare well. Science does much better.

But as the line of thought in this chapter suggests, this is not the right way to think about the relationship between science and religion. It is not quite right to say that science and religion are straightforwardly compatible or straightforwardly incompatible. For on the one hand, it is true that religion has a cosmological component, which I have just described. Someone could reasonably take the totality of modern scientific knowledge to be a reason to reject that component—there is no unseen order; the world is just not like that. This rejection is not, in the style of Russell's remark, one of the tenets of modern science itself but rather a metaphysical interpretation of the findings of science. On the other hand, the styles of thinking involved in science and religion are so different that it undermines the idea that there is a straightforward conflict between them. This is why it is also not unreasonable for a scientist well informed about the state of scientific knowledge also to endorse the religious impulse. It is a plain fact that many competent and even brilliant scientists are religious. And obviously they are not barred from being scientists—their work is not undermined—because of this.

Scientific explanation demands a very specific and technical kind of knowledge. It requires training, patience, specialization, a narrowing of focus, and (in the case of the most profound scientific theories) considerable mathematical knowledge and ability. No one can understand quantum theory—by all accounts, the most successful physical theory there has ever been—unless they grasp the underlying mathematics. Those who say otherwise are fooling themselves.

Religious belief is very different from this. It is not restricted only to those with a certain education or knowledge, it does not require years of training, it is not specialized, and it is not technical. I must emphasize here that I am talking about the religion of ordinary believers: the content, as I understand it, of what people who regularly attend church, mosque, or synagogue take themselves to be thinking. I'm not talking about the more complex technical ideas of theology or the way theologians interpret the content of ordinary belief.

Another difference between science and religion is that while religious belief is widespread, scientific knowledge is not. In fact, a rather small proportion of the world's seven billion people are actually interested in the details of contemporary scientific theories. Why? One obvious reason is that many lack the education to allow them to have access to this knowledge. Another reason is that even when they have access, these theories require sophisticated knowledge and abilities, which not everyone is capable of acquiring. Yet another reason, I would conjecture, is that most people aren't deeply interested in science, even when they have the opportunity to learn about it and the basic intellectual capacity to understand it. Of course, many (perhaps most) educated people who know about science know roughly what Einstein, Newton, and Darwin said. Many educated people accept the modern scientific view of the world and understand its main outlines. But this is not the same as being interested in the details of scientific research or being immersed in scientific thinking.

This lack of interest in science contrasts sharply with the worldwide interest in (or commitment to) religion. As we have already noted, religion commands and absorbs the passions and intellects of billions of people, many more people than have any interest in science. Why is this? Is it because—as the New Atheists would argue— many religious people want to explain the world in a scientific kind of way, but since they have not been properly educated, they haven't quite gotten there yet? Or is it because so many people are incurably irrational and are incapable of scientific thinking? Or is something else going on?

One answer to these questions, as we saw, is to reject the idea that religion deals in the factual at all. On a conception of religion that treats it as being about living a certain kind of value-infused life and seeing significance in the world, religion is a moral and practical outlook that is worlds away from scientific explanation. But I have already rejected this conception of religion. I have argued that it is absolutely essential to religions that they make certain factual or historical claims. "There is no God but Allah and Muhammad is his prophet" is a factual claim. And when Saint Paul says, "If Christ is not risen, then our preaching is in vain and our faith is in vain," he is saying that the point of his faith rests on certain facts, in particular a certain historical occurrence. Theologians will debate exactly what it means to claim that Christ has risen and what exactly the meaning and significance of this occurrence is, and they will give more or less sophisticated accounts of it. But all I am saying here is that whatever its specific nature,

Christians must hold that there was such an occurrence.

Let's return to the contrast with hypotheses. We saw that science involves forming hypotheses about the causes and natures of things in order to explain the phenomena we observe around us and to predict their future behavior. Some sciences—medical science, for example—make hypotheses about the causes of diseases and test them by intervening. Others—cosmology, for example—make hypotheses that are more remote from everyday causes and involve a high level of mathematical abstraction and idealization. Scientific reasoning involves an obligation to hold a hypothesis only to the extent that the evidence requires it. Scientists should not accept hypotheses that are ad hoc—that is, that are tailored for one specific situation but that cannot be generalized to others. Most scientific theories involve some kind of generalization: they don't just make claims about one thing but rather about things of a general kind. And their hypotheses are designed, on the whole, to make predictions; if these predictions don't come out true, then this is something for the scientists to worry about.

I argued previously that religions do not construct hypotheses in this sense. The fact that

Christianity rests on certain historical claims, like the claim of the resurrection, is not enough to make scientific hypotheses central to Christianity, any more than scientific hypotheses are central to the study of history. One can be an atheist because one rejects the historical basis of Christianity, but this is not the same as thinking that Christian doctrines are just bad hypotheses in the scientific sense.

Taken as scientific or proto-scientific hypotheses, religious claims fare pretty badly: they are ad hoc, they are arbitrary, they rarely make predictions, and when they do they almost never come true. Yet once again the striking fact is that it typically does not worry Christians when this happens. In the Gospels Jesus predicts the imminent end of the world and the coming of the kingdom of God. It does not worry believers that Jesus was actually wrong. If Jesus were framing something like a scientific hypothesis, then it should worry them. Critics of religion might say that this just shows the manifest irrationality of religion. But what I think it shows is that something other than hypothesis formation is going on.

Religious belief tolerates a high degree of mystery and ignorance in its understanding of the world, to an extent that would be inexplicable if it were a hypothesis-forming endeavor. When the devout pray and their prayers are not answered, they do not take this as evidence that has to be weighed alongside all the other evidence that prayer is effective. They generally feel no obligation to weigh the evidence. If God does not answer their prayers, well, there must be something that accounts for this, even though we may never know what it is. Why do people suffer if an omnipotent God loves them? Many complex answers have been offered, but in the end they come down to this: it's a mystery, a painful and troubling mystery.

Science too has its share of mysteries (or, rather, things that must simply be accepted without further explanation). But one aim of science is to minimize such things, to reduce the number of primitive concepts or primitive explanations. The religious attitude is very different. It does not seek to minimize mystery. Mysteries are accepted as a consequence of what, for the religious, makes the world meaningful.

This is the heart of the difference between science and religion. Religion is an attempt to make sense of the world, but it does not try to do this in the way science does. Science makes sense of the world by showing how things conform to its hypotheses. The characteristic mode of scientific explanation is showing how events fit into a general pattern. Religious explanation is not like this. At its most abstract, religious explanation does not have the scientific pattern, "X happened because there is a general regularity in the world, of the form Y." It's more like, "X happened. Accept it. Try to understand it." As Pascal Boyer points out, we should not assume that religion had its origin in the desire for the kind of explanation that science provides. Of all the kinds of things that we count as explanations, modern scientific explanation is only one.

I observed that while religious thinking is widespread in the world, scientific thinking is not. This fact should not be accounted for merely in terms of the ignorance or irrationality of those people who do not think scientifically. Rather, it is because the kind of intellectual, emotional, and practical appeal that religion has for people is a very different appeal from that which science has. Stephen Jay Gould once argued that religion and science are what he called "non-overlapping magisteria."[18] If he meant by this that religion makes no factual claims, then he is wrong. Claims about the transcendent, about the unseen order, and about the creation of the world are factual claims. They may not be scientifically provable or refutable—that is not at all a clear-cut matter. But if he meant that religion and science are very different kinds of attempts to understand the world, then Gould was certainly right: the search for meaning is a very different thing from the search for scientific knowledge.

Hypotheses, then, are not central to religious belief—what is central is the commitment to the meaningfulness of the world. But the commitment to this search for meaning is not always something that makes the world easier to understand or to cope with. In fact, it can make the world harder to understand—this is one lesson we can draw from the problem of inexplicable suffering and evil. The believer takes on an extra burden in trying to reconcile the existence of a loving God with evil, a burden that the atheist does not have. Trying to understand the extent of human suffering in a meaningful world is something with which the believer struggles—and from the outside, the struggle can seem a tragic failure.

This is where faith comes into the picture. I described one broad form of religious explana-

tion as "X happened. Accept it. Try to understand it." The attitude of accepting before trying
to understand it is summed up in Saint Anselm's
famous motto, *Credo ut intelligam*—I believe so
that I may understand. This is the attitude of
faith. Faith is not simply belief, in the sense introduced in Chapter 1. It is rather a kind of commitment to a worldview, through thick and thin;
one sticks to one's worldview rather in the way
that a faithful friend sticks with you in good
times and bad. Francis Spufford has nicely described how living a life of faith often has as
many bad times as good:

You ask for help and you get nothing: on a conscious
level you may have decided that there was nobody
there to help, but less consciously, since you did
ask, it feels as if help was denied. Hence the angry
edge that sometimes sharpens disbelief when it's
been renewed by one of these episodes of fruitless
asking. In the words of Samuel Beckett, "He doesn't
exist, the bastard!" The life of faith has just as many
he-doesn't-exist-the-bastard moments as the life of
disbelief. Probably more of them, if anything, given
that we believers tend to return to the subject more
often, producing many more opportunities to be
disappointed.[19]

The sense of feeling abandoned that the faithful can often give expression to—"My God my God, why hast thou forsaken me?"—is one reason it is wrong to see faith as a kind of intellectual self-satisfaction, as if it were the same thing as epistemic certainty. Indeed, Søren Kierkegaard went so far as to define faith and truth together in terms of "an objective *uncertainty* held fast in passionate inwardness."[20] It is also equally wrong to say, as some do, that the confidence of scientists in the truth of their own theories is itself a kind of faith. It's something entirely different.

Conceiving faith as dogmatic intellectual confidence would make a puzzle of some obvious features of religious belief—for example, funeral rites. And yet these features are surely not so puzzling. Some of the most powerful and compelling rites of all major religions arise out of the response to death, and even atheists can often be moved by these rites. But if believers had the dogmatic certainty that New Atheists sometimes attribute to them, the solemnity and sadness of funeral rites would be very puzzling. In those religions with a doctrine of the afterlife, why don't believers simply celebrate when their loved ones are taken away from them? Why the grieving, the lamenting, the dark and deep requiems?

The answer is that faith is not certainty but something more like a committed struggle to understand in the face of the palpable mystery of the world—what John Caputo has described, on St Augustine's behalf, as "the restless searching heart in the midst of a mysterious world."[21] But this inevitably makes unavailable the kind of unproblematic solace in the face of death that many atheists think is part of the point of religious belief ("the vast moth-eaten musical brocade / Created to pretend we never die"). There is a common idea that people believe because it will enable them to survive death—but the reality is that believers face the deprivation of bereavement in the same way others do. True, they may talk about the next world and the afterlife and mean it sincerely, but this is as much an expression of hope as any kind of explicit metaphysical supposition. For this reason Philip Kitcher is quite right when he says that "when religion retreats to confessing that the transcendent is a mystery, only apprehensible through figurative suggestions, its advertised power to bring comfort dissolves."[22]

Kitcher's point is that something is lost when we move from the literal to the figurative—certain forms of consolation that seemed available are no longer so. But this "retreat" should not be thought of as a contingent shortcoming of religious belief—as if the faithful were just looking for the final literal piece of the puzzle, the "grand unified theory" that would remove the need for figurative expression. Rather, it is a consequence of the fact that religion is *essentially* a struggle: to reconcile what can be explicit and what cannot be expressed, between what is mysterious about the world and what is clearly known. This struggle is not something that results from the incompleteness of religious belief, as the mystery in science might derive from the incompleteness of some theory or from the fact that we don't know enough. Rather, it derives from the very nature of the various human attempts to encounter what I am calling the transcendent. I know of no better expression of this predicament than that given in this remarkable passage from Alfred North Whitehead:

Religion is the vision of something which stands beyond, behind and within the passing flux of immediate things; something which is real, and yet waiting to be realised; something which is a remote possibility and yet the greatest of present facts; something that gives meaning to all that passes and yet eludes apprehension; something whose possession is the final good and yet is beyond all reach; something which is the ultimate ideal, and the hopeless quest.[23]

Not only do Whitehead's words express the paradoxicality of religious belief; they also show how utterly different the religious impulse is from science or any other epistemic endeavor. Any adequate account of religious belief must recognize this difference.

3

Identification

It is one thing to say what the essence of religion as a whole is, and another to say what distinguishes different religions from each another. In aiming to describe the content of a given religion, it is natural to turn to its principles, rules, or laws. Thus different forms of Christianity might be characterized in terms of the canon law of the Catholic Church or the thirty-nine articles of the Anglican Church, or summed up in the Apostles' Creed or the Ten Commandments. The principles of Islam are embodied in the

Quran and in Sharia law, and they are sometimes epitomized in the Five Pillars of Islam.

As we have seen, New Atheist discussions tend to concentrate on the cosmological or metaphysical principles, the large-scale claims about the nature of the universe. Hence the centrality in Richard Dawkins's discussion of what he calls the God Hypothesis, and the centrality of arguments for and against the existence of God in his book *The God Delusion*. In Chapter 2, I argued that Dawkins's God Hypothesis both significantly underdescribes and misdescribes the cosmological content of religious belief. For one thing, it concentrates on the idea of creation by a "superintelligence"; but the cosmological content of religion need not be restricted to this, and it need not be as specific. More importantly, I claimed that to call the cosmological content of religion a "hypothesis" is very misleading. If a hypothesis is just any factual claim whatsoever, then it is a hypothesis to say that there is an unseen order. But a hypothesis in *science* is supposed to be something more than a factual claim. It's supposed to be something that explains the observable data, and from which predictions can be derived. These features, as we saw, are mostly lacking from the cosmological claims of religion.

But even once we have obtained a proper understanding of religion's cosmological claims, this will not be the whole story about religious principles, rules, or laws. For many of the principles just mentioned are not about cosmology at all. Rather, they are about how to live one's life. Take the Five Pillars of Islam. The first is that there is no God but Allah, and Muhammad is his prophet. This is without doubt a factual claim. But the other four are imperatives: Muslims must pray five times a day; they must give alms; they must fast in the period of Ramadan; and they must make the pilgrimage to Mecca (the hajj) once in their life.

Only one of the Five Pillars, then, is a cosmological belief: there is no god but Allah (though notice this says nothing about superintelligence or creation). The others are about how a Muslim should behave. Similarly, only one of the Ten Commandments ("Thou shalt have no other gods before me") is about the existence of God, and therefore cosmological—though yet again, it is not about creation or superintelligence. The rest of the commandments are about worship (no idols, keep the Sabbath) and about morality, or good and bad behavior (the prohibitions against killing, adultery, coveting the goods of others, and so on).

Of course, the Five Pillars and the Ten Commandments are just capsule summaries of some central parts of belief systems with a complex content and a complex history. Summaries should not be expected to contain the whole content of the system. And of course there is more cosmology in Christianity than what is contained in the Ten Commandments. After all, the first sentence of the Hebrew Bible is, "In the beginning, God created the heavens and the earth." But it is nonetheless deeply significant that the Ten Commandments and the Five Pillars are often chosen to be the capsule or thumbnail version of these religions. Why should these be the things that, in some sense, define the outline essences of the religions of the Old Testament and Islam? And what conclusion should we draw from this fact about the nature of religion as a whole?

A common atheist picture of religion is that it is a blend of cosmology and morality. The cosmology is expressed by something like Dawkins's God Hypothesis; and (in the case of Christianity at least) the morality involves commitment to something like the moral parts of the command-ments or the moral teachings of Jesus. In this picture, the link between the cosmology and the morality is made through the idea of the afterlife: we must behave well, according to the morality of the church or the Bible or the Qur-an, because if we do we will have eternal life in heaven with God, and if we don't we will have eternal damnation or punishment in hell. (Remember Daniel Dennett's definition of reli-gions as "social systems whose participants avow belief in a supernatural agent or agents whose approval is to be sought.")[1]

I am sure this atheist picture of the essence of religion will be familiar to many. It is common also among some of those atheists who are sym-pathetic to religion, as well as those who are not. Ronald Dworkin, for example, who is as sym-pathetic an atheist as a religious believer could wish for, writes,

The conventional theistic religions with which most of us are most familiar—Judaism, Christianity and Islam—have two parts: a science part and a value part. The science part offers answers to important factual questions about the birth and history of the universe, the origin of human life, and whether or not people survive their own death. That part de-clares that an all-powerful and all-knowing God created the universe. . . . The value part of a con-ventional theistic religion offers a variety of convic-tions about how people should live and what they should value.[2]

Dworkin's picture contains a germ of truth—there is a distinction to be made between a reli-gion's views about cosmology and its views about how one should live. But calling the first the "science" part and second the "value" part is mis-leading, since it suggests that religion is just the combination of cosmology and morality. This both distorts and ignores some central features of religion and religious belief.

To see why, look at the examples I have just mentioned. Which of the noncosmological pil-lars of Islam have anything to do with what Dworkin calls its "science part" or with its "value part"? Certainly, that there is no God but Allah is a cosmological claim; and giving alms to help the needy is a moral act if anything is. But what about the pilgrimage, the fasting, and the praying? Are these part of morality in the normal sense of the word? Surely not—morality, what-ever else it is, is a matter of how one treats others. It is about right and wrong action. The injunctions to go on pilgrimage, to fast, and to pray are injunctions about how to live, in a broad sense, but they are not moral injunctions. Not every precept or principle relating to how to behave is a moral precept or principle.

Things are the same when we consider some of the defining practices of Judaism: keeping the Sabbath, keeping kosher, the circumcision of young boys. Although doctrinal and ritual traditions in Judaism differ widely, these are the elements that are common to them all. But none of them are about morality or cosmology.

It might be thought that Christianity fits more neatly into the cosmology-plus-morality picture. It is certainly true that even if they don't contain much cosmology, the Ten Commandments attempt to regulate moral behavior rather strictly: no stealing, adultery, or killing, and none of that coveting. But where do keeping holy the Sabbath and having no "graven images" fit into the cosmology-plus-morality picture? These practices seem to belong to neither category.

Moving beyond the Bible, consider the idea of a sacrament, an essential part of some Christian sects. A sacrament is a manifestation of God's grace in the world, where grace is defined in various ways; for example, in terms of the benevolence and mercy shown by God toward the human race. There are seven sacraments: baptism, confession, the Eucharist, confirmation, marriage, holy orders, and the sacrament of the sick, also known as the last rites (or "extreme unction"). Some of these are performed in a believer's life only once (baptism and confirmation being the uncontroversial examples) and some on a regular basis (confession and the Eucharist). But none of them have much to do with morality in the usual sense of that word. Nor are they, in any straightforward sense, mere expressions of cosmological belief. Rather, they are sui generis religious practices: a third category outside theories of cosmology or moral precepts.

What the cosmology-plus-morality picture leaves out, then, is something that seems absolutely central to the religions I am considering here: *religious practice*. Being a believer essentially involves doing certain things, performing certain activities, either once in one's life (baptism, confirmation, the hajj) or on a regular, repeated basis (ritual prayers, giving alms, the Sabbath). These activities are absolutely fundamental to anything that we recognize as a religion, but they are neither matters of morality nor simply the straightforward expression of some cosmological belief. This is why the cosmology-plus-morality picture of religion is so inadequate. It does not account for religious practice.

RITUAL AND BELONGING

But what exactly is religious practice, and how is it connected with what I am calling the religious impulse? To answer this question, we first need to reflect on two obvious and often overlooked features of such practices: the fact that believers generally don't invent religious practices themselves; and the fact that they participate in practices together with other people. Of course, there is private prayer and private worship, and there is inspiration and spontaneous invention. But the paradigm of religious practice is repetition—doing something that has been done before many times—and doing it socially, along with other people. These are not incidental or accidental features of religion but things that lie at its very heart: together they belong to what I call the element of identification.

Identification with a group is what connects the two features of religious practice: its repetitiousness and its social character. In principle, it is possible for these two things to be separated: people might gather spontaneously, utter words, and perform some kind of ceremony together, even if these things had never been said or done before. (Perhaps Pentecostals speaking in tongues is an example of this kind of thing.) And it would be possible for someone to repeat some ritual actions and words to themselves, on their own, independently of all others—though I can't think of a real, convincing example of this. But in religion as we mostly find it, it is crucial that the words believers recite have been said before many, many times, and that they have been said together by members of a group. This is why the identification with a group—a church, or faith, or sect—is an essential element of religious belief.

In saying this, I am merely putting in different words something that was said by Émile Durkheim over a hundred years ago. In his classic work *The Elementary Forms of Religious Life,* Durkheim emphasizes that the believers do not only embrace religious beliefs; they also *belong* to a church or religious group: "Religious beliefs proper are always held by a defined collectivity that professes them and practises the rites that go with them."[3] For Durkheim, this is what distinguishes religion from magic. Magical belief can manifest itself in rites and involves appeal to the supernatural. But "magic does not bind its followers to one another and unite them in a single group living the same life. *A church of magic does not exist.*"[4]

Some anthropologists, who, reasonably enough, want to stress the variety of religious belief and practice across the world, are happy to classify practices as religious that Durkheim would have classified as magical. Thus Pascal Boyer discusses beliefs and practices relating to witches that are still common in some parts of Africa, alongside the allegiance to forms of Christianity.[5] Of course it is possible to classify things in this way, grouping together religious beliefs with other supernatural beliefs and superstitions, and call the whole lot "religion." But this classification deliberately ignores the distinction Durkheim was aiming at, and it seems to me this distinction is of the greatest importance. For without it, we cannot understand why religion dominates all aspects of believers' lives, in a way that magic does not.

Genuinely religious practice must involve membership or belonging. Membership is made possible either by some initiation rite or by being born into the relevant group. For many people, then, belonging to a religion is similar to belonging to a nation or having an ethnicity. In the normal course of events, one chooses neither one's ethnicity nor one's nationality. One can renounce citizenship, but citizenship is not the same thing as nationality. Nationality and religion differ in many ways, but I think the comparison between the two is useful in illustrating what kind of belonging is at issue here.

In its broadest outlines, the phenomenon of identification is a quite general human phenomenon, not restricted to religious believers. But the ways it manifests itself in religious and national identification are in some aspects similar and in some aspects different.

People do not necessarily identify with their nation or their nationality. They can attempt to detach themselves from it, and many are successful at doing this. But when they do identify, this results in what I would call patriotism. Patriotism as I mean it is not a belief in the superiority of one's own country, or the belief that one's own country should triumph over all others. (We could introduce by stipulation the term "nationalism" for these often more dangerous ideas.) It is rather a matter of identifying with your country *as yours.* This can show itself in pride for your country, but it is equally important that it can show itself in shame too. The same can happen with religions—the liberal Catholic milieu in which I was educated was full of Catholics who agonized about the role of the church in the world and felt a particular kind of shame about its doings, a shame that would not be felt by those who merely criticized the church from the outside. Mere disapproval or blame does not imply shame.

In discussions of patriotism, you sometimes encounter the view that you cannot be proud of your country because you can only be proud of something you have yourself achieved—maybe even "by definition." But this isn't true: when people are proud of what their children do, this is not because they think of their children as in some sense their own achievement. There might be people who think like this, but this would surely be a narcissistic and perverted form of parental love. Genuine love for your children is not self-directed, nor is genuine pride in their achievements. Similarly, pride in your country might take a more or less self-satisfied form, but it need not involve any belief that you were responsible for the things of which you are proud.

The point is even clearer, perhaps, in the case of shame—perhaps an emotion that some educated liberal Westerners are more willing to admit to feeling in relation to their own countries. Many liberal Americans who objected to the invasion of Iraq in 2003 did not simply express their objection in terms of disapproval or moral condemnation; many of them described themselves as feeling "ashamed to be American." It was the same in Britain. The slogan of the 2003 peace march in London—the largest ever public demonstration in Britain, attracting over a million people—was "Not in My Name." This is a distinct sentiment from condemnation or disapproval, although it implies it. Rather, the phrase expresses the protesters' feeling that they are somehow implicated in the shameful decision to go to war. This would be unintelligible if you could only feel shame for those things you had done, since it's safe to assume that none of the protesters had made that decision. Where the sense of shame comes from, I would argue, is the fact that the protesters identify with the country whose government made this decision.

I intend these remarks to illustrate how widespread and natural the phenomenon of identification is. I'm not saying that having a religion is the same as having a nationality, or an ethnicity or a gender. But there is this similarity: in identifying with your faith or church, you typically see it as part of what constitutes your identity. This is what it means to belong. In Roger Scruton's words, being a member of a religious faith is a matter of standing in "a network of relations that are neither contractual nor negotiated."[6]

Identification differs from the ideal of social and political integration offered by much contemporary liberal political philosophy. By "liberal political philosophy" I mean the attempt to derive the correct political system from reflection on the interrelations between the somewhat abstract concepts of justice, liberty, and democracy. The leading figure of liberal political philosophy in the twentieth and twenty-first centuries is, without question, the American philosopher John Rawls. Rawls treated justice as the central concept of politics, where "justice" refers not to what the law courts dispense (known as "retributive justice") but to the correct allocation or distribution of resources by the state ("distributive justice"). Rawls argued for two principles of justice. The first is that everyone has a claim to the same basic liberties;

the second is that any inequalities can only be justified if they are to the benefit of the worst off, and they should only be the result of processes that involve equality of opportunity.

Rawls used an ingenious thought experiment to derive this complex relationship between liberty, equality, and fairness. He asked us to imagine which principles we would choose to govern a fair society if we did not know which position we would occupy in it. He argued that behind such a "veil of ignorance," we would choose principles that maximized a fair distribution of resources in society.

The approach pioneered by Rawls could be called "rationalistic" in the sense that it treats the correct form of political life to be determined by something like an idealized rational contract governed by universal and abstract principles. What such rationalist philosophy has difficulty in finding a place for is the centrality of those convictions, attachments, and commitments we have that cannot be derived from, or justified in terms of, any kind of principle of justice or fairness, or anything like a rational contract. These commitments come from belonging to the social groups we do, from the responsibilities we feel ourselves to have that are part of what Martin Heidegger called our "thrownness" *(Geworfenheit)*—the fact that we are "thrown" into a world that is not of our own making. For good or ill, some of our most fundamental ways of engaging with the world derive from this fact.[7]

Take the family, for example. We do not choose our families, and yet we have commitments and bonds to our family members that are deeper and more real to us than many of the commitments we explicitly and knowledgeably sign up for (employment contracts, for instance). Family relationships are a paradigm of what Scruton calls "a network of relations that are neither contractual nor negotiated." It is perhaps not surprising, then, that Rawls and his followers have had difficulty fitting the family into their systems of justice, since the family is plainly not a place of equal opportunity and so contravenes the second principle of justice. As Rawls put it, "The principle of fair opportunity can be only imperfectly carried out, at least as long as the institution of the family exists."[8]

This point about the family is actually related to a familiar New Atheist criticism of religion: that religion indoctrinates children and imposes religious worldviews on them before they are able to choose to be Jewish, Muslim, or Christian. A. C. Grayling, for example, has claimed that most of the religious are those in whom "supernatural beliefs and superstitions were inculcated as children when they could not assess the value of what they were being sold as a world view."[9] This criticism assumes that belonging to a religion is ideally a choice that should be made as a rational decision, in full view of the facts, as it were. But in fact such a form of belonging is supposed to be much more like other things that one inherits when growing up in a family: how to eat together, how to behave with guests and strangers, how to talk to your elders, whom to obey and when, and all the other norms and values that govern how we live together as families.

Of course, there are differences, as there are with nationality and ethnicity. In many societies, one can renounce one's religion, just as one can renounce one's family and one's citizenship. Grayling and others surely exaggerate when they describe all religious ideas as being implanted into helpless children as if they cannot ever be removed—though the image helps their case rhetorically in explaining why it is that so many millions of adults do not reject the religions into which they were born. But my main point is that these attachments are, in their different ways, part of our thrownness as human beings rather than a result of some rational choice. In this way, belonging to a religion is less like belonging to a political party and more like belonging to a family. So the critics are correct to point out that children brought up as religious do not do so freely. But this limitation on their freedom is of a similar kind to those restrictions that come with belonging to a family. Children do not choose the moral or behavioral norms imposed on them by their parents, and many try to escape them. But whether desirable or not, it is impossible to imagine how the institution of the family could exist without the imposition of some such norms.

These remarks are not intended as a justification of the practice of bringing up children in a certain religion. My point is only to emphasize that this practice is not some peculiar perversity of religious indoctrination but rather something of the same kind as many practices that arise out of human thrownness. This fact also illustrates that identification with a religious group need not involve a conscious decision, although it may do so. It does, however, involve dividing the world—into Catholics and non-Catholics,

Jews and Gentiles, Muslims and non-Muslims, the saved and the damned . . . the in-group and the out-group. (Here the difference with the belief in magic is quite clear again.) This is another aspect of religion that attracts criticism: the division of humanity into exclusive groups is claimed to be one of the sources of conflict, violence, and atrocity. I will address the question of religion's role in violence and atrocity in Chapter 4.

The identification with an inside group rather than an outside group seems essential to all religions. But this identification is pretty empty if it is not accompanied by religious practice. Some element of identification can remain among those who participate in no religious practices whatsoever; this is the sentiment expressed by those who say they remain Catholic even if they have not gone to church for decades. But it's not clear how seriously we should take such claims. The fact is that, for your identification with a religious group to constitute a *religious* identification, you must go to church, temple, mosque, or synagogue. Then you will participate in the ritual, routine activities that are common to that group as a whole. Doing what the group does is not some dispensable extra—it is absolutely central to religious belief.

Notice too, though, that the comparison with other forms of identification holds here too. Belonging to a society involves conforming to a wide range of norms and codes of behavior. Some of these are explicitly learned, and others you pick up by a kind of social osmosis when young. One of the aims of this book is to try to shift the atheist's conception of religion away from it being seen as something anomalous in human society, and therefore something that can be, and should be, removed without leaving much of a scar. My view is closer to Durkheim's: human society is religious through and through, both in terms of what human habits and structures it involves and in terms of what traces religious ideas have left in even the most secular societies.

It is very easy for highly educated Westerners to overlook the importance of belonging, even when it might not appear that this is what is really going on. Consider, for example, one familiar aspect of the New Atheist alternative to religious belief: its devotion to science and the value of scientific knowledge. Dawkins and others frequently (and correctly) emphasize that an enormous amount of meaning and satisfaction can be gained from scientific endeavor itself. We can find meaning in our discovery that the world is a beautiful place, and in understanding the principles that make it work. Dawkins writes passionately,

The feeling of awed wonder that science can give us is one of the highest experiences of which the human psyche is capable. It is a deep aesthetic passion to rank with the finest that music and poetry can deliver. It is truly one of the things that makes life worth living.[10]

Let's put to one side the question of whether this is really the kind of thing that would satisfy those searching for the kind of meaning that religious belief can bring. (I doubt this myself, for the reasons given in Chapter 1.) What I want to emphasize here instead is how this capacity to find meaning through science is often itself a fundamentally communal matter, relying on the existence of a community of inquirers with similar values, values with which scientists can identify. I owe this point to Philip Kitcher:

Thoroughly secular societies can contain structures enabling people to enter into sympathetic relations with one another, to achieve solidarity with their fellows, to exchange views about topics that concern them most, to work together to identify goals that matter to all members of the group and to pursue those ends through cooperative efforts. Authors of contemporary manifestos calling for freedom from religious delusions typically belong to professional communities. . . . Taking that for granted, the lack of similar secular structures for others disappears from their view. Focused on adding to the stock of factual truths and finding an entirely reasonable satisfaction in sharing that goal with their closest colleagues, they want the delight of apprehending factual truth to be shared by all . . . and so they see purifying progress, the replacement of factually false religious doctrines with clear-headed denial, as a major advance for humanity. In many parts of the affluent world, however, particularly in the United States, there are no serious opportunities, outside the synagogues and churches and mosques, for fellowship with all the dimensions religious communities can provide.[11]

Kitcher brings out nicely how immersion in your own lifestyle can blind you to the features that allow you to get satisfaction from activities such as pursuing scientific knowledge for its own sake. Belonging to an academic community (for example, a university) might seem to you to be useful but inessential to the value that this pursuit brings to your life. And certainly it is true that people can pursue knowledge outside any formal communal framework—something that is becoming easier and easier in the age of the Internet. But nonetheless, it is worth reflecting seriously on how you might really go about the pursuit of knowledge without the structure and support of a community of like-minded individuals—something many of the New Atheists have easy access to. You share your ideas with others who have similar goals; they explain things to you and you to them; you attend meetings with intelligent, educated people who appreciate what you are doing; you publish in highly regarded academic periodicals and journals; you gain respect and praise for your work; and so on. The search for knowledge that Dawkins and others (rightly) prize so highly is something that takes place within a very robust and sophisticated social framework; and for many people, it surely derives some of its value from its location in that framework. How might science be able to give meaning to scientists' lives if they do not belong to a community of scientists? This seems to me a very good question, and the answer to it is not obvious.

Institutions acquire much of the meaning they have for us over long periods of time. It takes time for the occurrence of a practice within an institution to be something that we value. Religious institutions are paradigms in this respect. As I mentioned at the beginning of this section, in the most central religious traditions, certain practices—the words you utter, the ritual actions you perform—typically have a long history. But why is this fact so important for religious communities? To my mind, there are at least two reasons. The first is that saying the prayers that have been passed down through the years is a way of connecting you with your religious community in the past in a common quest for significance. Once again this is similar to other social practices in which repetition is frequently very important. The things we say before we eat or when we meet each other, what we do when we enter someone else's house—things that are so familiar to us that we scarcely notice them— are acts of repetition that give a structure to everyday communal experience.

There are cases, of course, in which religious revolutions attempt to overturn the rituals that have been performed for decades or centuries and replace them with superior, often "purified," rituals. The Protestant Reformation is an obvious example. And some movements aim for the "renewal" of the believer through baptism or being "born again." Pentecostalism, with over five hundred million adherents around the world, is a good example—and some Pentecostal meetings involve only spontaneous preaching and "speaking in tongues." So we should not say of absolutely every religion that it can only use words and ceremonies that have been used before—for, after all, these rituals have to start somewhere! But notice also that it is often a significant fact about religious revolutions that they aim to *return* to some earlier, more pure or original version of a doctrine—this is particularly true of Pentecostalism.

The second reason that the words believers utter often have a long history is that the repetition of these words—often strange, archaic, and only partially understood—is an attempt to link them not only with past worshippers and other members of their religion but also with something beyond the quotidian: what I am calling the transcendent. Rituals in which special words are uttered or sung are common to every religious tradition. These words are supposed to connect not only back to the tradition to which the believers belong but also outward, as it were, to the hidden, unseen order beyond this experience. This aspect of religious practice will be our key to understanding how the two essential elements of religious belief—the religious impulse and identification—fit together, as I shall now attempt to explain.

THE SACRED

It is important to acknowledge, to begin with, that the two elements of religious belief can come apart in the lives of individual religious believers. There can be people who have the religious impulse but do not participate in any practices; and there can be people who participate but lack any sense of the transcendent, or any interest in pursuing it. But my claim is that in full religious belief and in the religious traditions I am considering here, they go together.

Why is this? What is the connection between the two elements of religious belief? Is there some kind of conceptual or intelligible link between them, or is it just a contingent historical mess? My answer is that the link between the religious impulse and identification is made by the idea of the sacred. The idea that the sacred is what characterizes religion is again familiar from Durkheim's work. Durkheim observed that the distinction between sacred things and nonsacred ("profane") things is central to all religions, and he defined a religion as a "unified system of beliefs and practices relative to sacred things."[12]

Durkheim's discussion of the sacred, over one hundred years old, remains one of the most fertile discussions of religion. Sacred things, Durkheim points out, are not necessarily those "personal beings we call gods or spirits." Anything at all can be sacred: "a rock, a tree, a spring, a stone, a piece of wood, a house."[13] Sacred things do not have to be concrete material objects: words, speeches, and formulas that have been uttered by countless people over the centuries are among the most familiar sacred objects.

Durkheim thought that sacred things are those that are "set apart and surrounded by prohibitions."[14] The prohibitions concern the way in which a sacred thing must not be treated "as though it belonged in the ordinary frame of nature," in Scruton's words.[15] To do this is profanation; or worse, desecration. But this is not because sacred things are treated as in some way more "powerful" or magnificent or grand than profane things. As Durkheim observes, believers can feel very comfortable and "at home" with sacred things (amulets, crucifixes, rosaries, and so on). What is essential, though, is that the distinction between the sacred and the profane is absolute, exclusive, and exhaustive. If an individual thing, or a type of thing, is sacred, then it cannot also be profane, and vice versa. Durkheim says that sacred and profane things have "nothing in common," but this more extreme claim is unnecessary. If a church building is deconsecrated, it is, in the most important sense, no longer a church, but it has plenty in common with the thing that was (the stones from which it was made, for example). But if something *is* a church, then that thing itself (as opposed to some of its parts) cannot also be profane. And there is nothing that is neither sacred nor profane.

We can understand these points by taking an example from the list Durkheim mentions—a building or a house. The most sacred site (and the most sacred object) in Islam is the Kaaba in Mecca: a small cuboid building thirteen meters tall. The Kaaba predates Muhammad (who lived around 600 BC), and obscurity surrounds its origins. It is variously called the House of Allah, the House of Worship, or the Sacred House. All Muslims must direct themselves toward the Kaaba when they pray; the required hajj pilgrimage involves walking around the Kaaba with other pilgrims in a counterclockwise direction.

Considered as a material object, the Kaaba is a fairly ordinary, though beautiful, thing. But its role in Islam makes it utterly unique. Every day hundreds of millions of people think of themselves as directed toward Mecca and therefore this object when they pray. If asked to explain the significance of something like the Kaaba in the terms that are intelligible to those in the Western atheist intellectual tradition, some people may be tempted to treat it as an object of superstition, or perhaps as something perceived as having magical powers. A magical object is something with powers to bring about changes in the world that have no possible scientific explanation. Magical objects have something special about them, in and of themselves.

Sacred objects like the Kaaba are not the same thing as magical objects, in any sense. Consider the most familiar of sacred objects: the sacred text. The People of the Book (Jews, Christians, and Muslims) focus their ritual and religious practice on texts that are revered as sacred: the Torah, the Bible, and the Quran. These objects are sacred in two dimensions, so to speak. On the one hand, there are the actual words themselves, the abstract text that can be spoken or written and so is independent of individual copies of these books. On the other hand, there are the individual, material copies of the books themselves. The uttering of the sacred words plays a role in prayer and rites, and these collections of words themselves are regarded as sacred. Hence oaths and profane language. But individual material copies of the texts are sacred too, as is shown by the fact that they can be desecrated. For a copy of a sacred text to be burned, spat on, or otherwise defiled can be a genuinely distressing and offensive thing to a believer.

There is no parallel to desecration in the case of magical objects. And it is no part of genuine religious belief that the sacred text has magical powers. No orthodox Christian thinks that the sacred significance of the Bible lies in the fact that it can be used to do things that contravene the laws of nature, in the way magical objects are supposed to. It is important to repeat the point, made already in this chapter, that we miss something very significant about the essence of religion if we see its essential feature as what it has in common with magic—"the supernatural."

What is this important thing? This is how I will put it: sacred objects play two roles in religious practice, what I will call their "internal" role and their "external" role. The internal role is to be the bearers of religious meaning inside and outside a religious ritual. The crucifix, the scrolls of the Torah, the Kaaba itself—these objects are essential to rituals themselves in the sense that it is not possible for the rituals to be what they are without the involvement of these objects. They also frequently function as a way of connecting the rest of the believer's life with the sacred. This is why, during prayer, Orthodox Jews wear leather boxes strapped to their arms (known as phylacteries or tefillin) containing parchment with verses from the Torah, and some Christians will wear a crucifix all the time. These objects illustrate what Karen Armstrong has called the religious ambition to "bring the whole of human life into the ambit of the sacred."[16] This is because of their meaning, or what philosophers call their *intentionality*—the fact that they point beyond the mere material reality to the desired transcendent reality beyond. As Scruton puts it,

Sacred objects, words, animals, ceremonies, places all seem to stand at the horizon of our world, looking out to that which is not of this world, because it belongs in the sphere of the divine, and looking also into our world, so as to meet us face-to-face.[17]

I describe it this way from the religious believer's point of view, of course; in my view, there is no transcendent reality. But this is what the sacred aims at, whether or not it exists. This is where the concept of intentionality is useful.

"Intentionality" in the philosophical sense, deriving from the work of the philosophers Franz Brentano and Edmund Husserl, is a word for the capacity of things (usually restricted to minds or states of mind) to be directed at things other than themselves. The intentionality of thoughts and beliefs is their representational power—the fact that every thought or belief is a thought *of* something or a belief *about* something. The intentionality of desire or hope consists in the fact that a desire or hope is a desire or hope *for* something; and similarly with other states of mind. One distinctive thing about intentionality is that this "directedness" can be directedness at something that does not exist. Whereas an arrow cannot be aimed at a target if there is no target there, a thought can be directed at an object even if that object does not exist, and a desire can be a desire for something even if there is no such thing.

The internal role of sacred objects is to point beyond themselves to the transcendent. The crucifix points toward the salvation of humanity that it represents, the sacrifice made by Jesus that believers take to be redeeming humanity from its sins. The Quran points in its precepts and commands to the will of Allah; the books of the Torah point toward the special role of the Jewish people as revealed in their history and their law. The internal meaning of these objects is always to indicate something about the transcendent unseen order, and their significance lies in the fact that they are part of the everyday world but point beyond it to something non-everyday that gives significance to everything. As Scruton says, they are at the "horizon of our world."

Atheists can coherently describe sacred objects in terms of their intentionality, their pointing beyond the everyday, even if they don't believe that there is anything to which these objects point. Indeed, the need for objects to point beyond the everyday is one of the most familiar and intelligible needs that religious practices and ceremonies attempt to answer. In a letter to a friend, the English historian Hugh Trevor-Roper described his dismay in finding himself at a secular funeral:

We stood silently around the coffin in the crematorium. No clergymen, no music, no articulate sound. Then suddenly the floor gaped and hey presto! The coffin sank out of sight. Whereupon we trooped silently away. I hope that my Doctorate of Divinity will at least save my corpse from such an undignified disposal: like waste going down the sink.[18]

The sardonic tone aside, Trevor-Roper is here expressing something that is a real need among the religious and the nonreligious alike: the need to mark the important moments of a life with something solemn and serious. Nowhere is this more apparent than in funeral rites; unsurprisingly, since the mystery of life emerges most poignantly and forcefully in our encounter with death. And even some atheists will feel the mystery of life at these moments: they were there, and now they are gone, never to be seen again. How can this be?

The second role of sacred things, which I call its external role, is to unify the members of a religion. Religions are united in their membership by its common commitment to the same catalogue of sacred things. This is how Durkheim defines a church: "a society whose members are united because they share a common conception of the sacred world and its relation to the profane world, and who translate this common conception into identical practices."[19] What binds a church or a religion together in this sense may be nothing more than commitment to the same sacred texts (think of the Pentecostals). Or it may involve some objects or types of objects (the Kaaba, the sacred cows of the Hindus). Again the contrast with magic is striking. Magic "does not bind its followers to one another and unite them in a single group living the same life," and "the magician has a clientele, not a church, and his clients may well be entirely unrelated and even unaware of each other; even their relations with him are generally accidental and transitory, like those of a patient to a doctor."[20]

The sacred, then, is what connects the two elements of religious belief that are the core themes of this book—the religious impulse and identification. Sacred things are objects that bind a religious community together, over time and at a time, in religious practices built around them; but they also point toward something beyond, toward the transcendent, however this is exactly conceived.

It should be clear from this discussion that those atheists who say they can preserve some idea of the sacred are either mistaken or using the word in a very different way.[21] Sometimes atheists attempt to claim that they too are entitled to the idea of sacred things. Simon Blackburn, for example, complains about the "religious appropriation of the sacred" and says that "to regard something as sacred is to see it as marking a boundary to what may be done."[22] That's true, but there are many ways in which boundaries can be drawn that do not mark out the sacred in any real sense—moral prohibitions or other taboos draw sharp boundaries between things to be done, but these are not the boundaries between the sacred and the profane. What atheists normally mean by this is that certain things are very precious or have some special kind of meaning or significance that goes beyond any pleasure or satisfaction given by them in the present moment. But the notion of the sacred that I have appealed to here, derived from Durkheim and later writers influenced by him, is something very different from this. It essentially involves religious practice or ritual and the intentional "pointing" toward the transcendent. There can be nothing like this in an atheist's world picture.

4

Religion and Violence

ATROCITY

At the height of the sectarian killings in Iraq in the middle of the first decade of the twenty-first century, between fifty and a hundred bodies a day were regularly found in the streets of Baghdad. In symbolic retaliation for Sunni atrocities, Shia killers would often leave the bodies of their Sunni victims in the craters left by Al-Qaeda car bombs. A favored method of killing was a power drill to the skull. One man who was widely credited with inflaming the ancient conflict in Iraq between Shia and Sunni Muslims, the murderous Abu Musab al-Zarqawi, was killed by a U.S. air strike in 2006. But his followers transformed themselves into the self-proclaimed Islamic State (IS). Since IS established itself in Syria and Iraq in 2014, it has beheaded, drowned, and burned its victims alive, frequently filming these killings for the world to view on the Internet.

What should students of religion say about this terrible state of affairs? How should they understand it? The questions are pressing for those who want to understand the role of religion in the world today, because many atheists see this dismal situation—and many others like it—as fundamentally religious in nature. Richard Dawkins is typical: "Iraq, as a consequence of the Anglo-American invasion of 2003, degenerated into sectarian civil war between Sunni and Shia Muslims. Clearly a religious conflict."[1] In recent years, so-called Islamist violence has dominated the political news across the world, and, indeed, it is arguable that the passion of some of the New Atheists can be explained in terms of their reaction to the Al-Qaeda terrorist attacks of September 11, 2001. But many of the antireligious are keen to emphasize that it is *religion,* rather than just Islam, that gives the deeper explanation of this evil, and I will take them at their word here. I will not discuss those who single out Islam as the uniquely violent religion, and I will not touch on the anti-Islamic comments made by some New Atheists or speculate about covert anti-Islamic motives among the others. I will here just discuss those who see religion as one source, or the major source, of the world's troubles. Islam is one case, but there is supposed to be the same pattern in other faiths. Thus Dawkins writes,

In Northern Ireland, Catholics and Protestants are euphemised to "Nationalists" and "Loyalists" respectively. . . . The original usage of "ethnic cleansing" in the former Yugoslavia is also arguably a euphemism for religious cleansing, involving Orthodox Serbs, Catholic Croats and Muslim Bosnians.[2]

In his well-known book *God Is Not Great,* Christopher Hitchens makes exactly the same points about these two cases.[3]

The recent atrocities are, for these writers, merely instances of a general pattern throughout human history. The violence and destruction imposed in the name of Christianity has a long history: the medieval Crusades; the Spanish Inquisition in the fifteenth century; the French

Wars of Religion in the sixteenth century; the Thirty Years' War (1618–1648), which reduced the population of central Europe by one-third and destroyed countless cities and settlements; the many massacres of Jews by Christians across the centuries; and we could go on, of course. Put like this, you can see why people say that the history of Europe in the second millennium AD was a history of religious violence.

Against this has to be placed the equally terrible history of large-scale nonreligious violence and cruelty. Examples easily spring to mind: the killing of the Central American natives by the conquistadores, the slave trade, the extermination of the Tasmanian aborigines by the British colonists, the massacre of the Armenians by the Turks in 1915, the slaughter of hundreds of thousands of Chinese by the Japanese at Nanking in 1937, the killing of over a million in the Rwandan genocide of 1994. And then of course there are the other monstrous crimes of the twentieth century: the Nazi Holocaust and the mass killings by the communist regimes in China and the Soviet Union. As with religious violence, it seems all too easy to find examples.

Some writers more sympathetic to religion attempt to argue that these examples show that religion is not really the source of the world's problems, and that even so-called religious conflicts are not really religious underneath. While not denying the links between religious groups and violence, Karen Armstrong traces the origin of human violence to the beginnings of agrarian societies and the accumulation of wealth; these things, she argues, and not religion as such, are much more important in explaining the predicament we are in.[4]

The account I sketched of identification in Chapter 3 of this book indicates one other place where an explanation of religious violence that is not specifically religious might begin. The tendency of human beings to form groups explicitly defined in opposition to others, which then seek the destruction and subordination of the other groups, is one of the characteristic features of many recognizably human societies. But facts like these do not mean that religion has no special, distinctively *religious* role in explaining episodes of violence. It would be entirely wrong to try to explain away or eliminate the role played by religion in igniting people's passions and leading them to the kinds of acts of violence described previously. The question is rather, what is this role?

The origins of each of the three monotheistic faiths are deeply entwined in violence in one way or another—in the myths of their foundation, in their actual histories, or both. At the beginning of the book of Genesis, the first significant human act after Adam's disobedience was the murder of Abel by his brother Cain. The early history of the Jews, as represented in the Hebrew Bible, is a history of massacre, exile, rape, and vengeance. Islam's beginning in violence is a matter not so much of what is recorded in its sacred texts but rather of its actual history. Muhammad's early struggles with the tribes in Arabia occasioned him to lead the massacre in 627 AD of seven hundred Jewish men of Qurayzah and to send the women and children of the tribe to be sold as slaves. Christianity has at its historical and spiritual heart the defining event of the crucifixion, an exceptionally vicious form of execution, spelled out and celebrated in gruesome detail in the texts and art of its tradition.

Given the violence at the heart of the monotheistic religions, it is perhaps not surprising that critics of religion should see its propensity to cause violence as one of the main things to be held against it. Hitchens argues that religion "poisons everything. As well as a menace to civilization, it has become a threat to human survival." Religion is "violent, irrational, intolerant, allied to racism, tribalism, and bigotry, invested in ignorance and hostile to free inquiry, contemptuous of women and coercive toward children," and sectarian, and that, accordingly, it "ought to have a great deal on its conscience."[5] Sam Harris goes even further, claiming that "a glance at history, or at the pages of any newspaper, reveals that ideas which divide one group of human beings from another, only to unite them in slaughter, generally have their roots in religion."[6] The idea that religion is the principal cause of the world's violence and suffering is a common theme in New Atheist writing. But it seems to me that this claim is a large exaggeration and does not survive either a careful scrutiny of the facts or a proper understanding of what makes a conflict religious.

First of all, we need to distinguish two broad (if somewhat vague) ideas. The first is the idea that like all human institutions, religious institutions and groups have throughout history been responsible for atrocities and have caused great suffering. The second is that religious institutions have been in some way uniquely responsible for the worst horrors and evils of the human race.

The first idea is obviously true, and the second obviously false. Anyone who wants to defend the second idea has to somehow account for the fact that among the worst horrors of human history were the stupendous crimes of the twentieth century. The communist regimes of Joseph Stalin (between 15 and 20 million killed) and Chairman Mao Zedong (at least 30 million killed) were in no sense religious. Nor was the Nazi regime, which was responsible for atrocities of such systematic viciousness and brutality that we still struggle today to make sense of them. On one measure of the worst—the sheer number of people killed, the gratuitous and random murders, the systematic and humiliating torture and extermination of whole groups, the terror-ization of the population—the nonreligious re-gimes of Stalin, Mao, and Adolf Hitler are clearly responsible for some of the worst atroc-ities in civilization. The second idea is simply unsustainable.

Some atheists respond to this familiar point by arguing that the communists were "really" reli-gious underneath. Harris writes,

Even when such crimes have been secular, they have required the egregious credulity of entire societies to be brought off. Consider the millions of people who were killed by Stalin and Mao: although these tyrants paid lip service to rationality, communism was little more than a political religion. . . . Even though their beliefs did not reach beyond this world, they were both cultic and irrational.[7]

We even find this kind of idea in those opposed to the New Atheists. John Gray is not one of those who blame religion for the world's problems, but he does claim that "Nazism and Communism were political religions, each with its ersatz shrines and rituals."[8]

The trouble with this way of thinking is that it can only reach its conclusion by a stipulation or a redefinition of the word "religion"—one of the things I have already objected to. But for the New Atheists in particular, this is not a consistent move, since they persistently criticize religions for their superstitious belief in a supernatural agency. Yet Stalinism, Nazism, and Maoism appeal to no supernatural agencies. So New Atheists can't hold both that the essence of religion is its belief in the supernatural *and* that its essence is merely cultic, dogmatic groupthink (even assuming this is a good description of Stalinism and Nazism—which it surely isn't). Worse than the inconsistency, though, is the vague and incorrect conception of religion appealed to here. I have argued in Chapters 2 and 3 that religion essentially involves two things: the religious impulse and identification. Without the first, we get mere belonging; and without the second, we get mere solitary mysticism. Not all rituals are religious rituals; not everything that religion's critics might call a "shrine" is really a shrine. Nothing in Nazism, Stalinism, or Maoism corresponds to what in actual religions is considered sacred. The idea that these systems of thought are in some sense "religions" is a superficial maneuver that adds little value to this debate.

Given the enormity of nonreligious atrocities both in and before the twentieth century, there is no point in pursuing the idea that religion has been responsible for the worst violence in human history. Should we then settle instead for the boring, unexceptional truth that religion has been responsible for some of the bad things but not for all? (Of course, if we agreed with Émile Durkheim that human society and religion grew up together, then blaming religion is closely related to blaming human society.) This banal claim is no doubt true, but it does raise more interesting questions: What does it mean to say that a conflict is religious at all? What is the role of religion in human conflict? It turns out that the answers to these questions are more complex than one might initially think.

THE ROLE OF RELIGION IN HUMAN CONFLICT

What are conflicts about? Can we have a general theoretical account of conflict? Many human conflicts are disputes among different groups about territory or the ownership of land or other property, or the dominance by force of one group by another. How does religion fit into a general picture of conflict?

We can begin to address these large and difficult questions by distinguishing a number of different kinds of answers. Religion's role in violent conflict has been said to derive from

1. the explicitly theological content of (theistic) religions;
2. nontheological elements of religious doctrines, such as rules about how to live or worship;

3. the element of identification, which I have argued is essential to religion;
4. aspects of human psychology, society, and culture that are not essentially religious.

With the exception of the appeal to (1), which has little to be said for it, my conclusion will be that what is called religious violence or conflict is normally some complex combination of (2), (3), and (4).

Let us first briefly put to one side the appeal to (1), the view that theological or cosmological views themselves have a major role in religious violence. It's not that no one has ever expressed such a view. Harris says that India and Pakistan "are now poised to exterminate one another with nuclear weapons simply because they disagree about 'facts' that are every bit as fanciful as the names of Santa's reindeer. . . . The only difference between these groups consists in what they believe about God."[9] Like many of Harris's polemical remarks, this is unsupportable. Whatever the truth about the basis of the conflict between India and Pakistan, theological beliefs had nothing to do with it. In Ramachandra Guha's comprehensive history of modern India, for example, theological beliefs are not mentioned once as playing any role in the violent history of India and Pakistan since partition.[10]

Of course, what Harris no doubt means is that *religion* is the basis of the conflict between India and Pakistan, because Pakistan is predominantly Muslim, and India largely Hindu. And because, like all the New Atheists, he equates religion with a collection of cosmological and theological beliefs, he treats "religion" and "beliefs about God" as the same thing. This equation of religion with beliefs about God is one of the mistakes I am arguing against in this book.

Nonetheless, it is worth asking whether there are any other cases in which people's beliefs about God—rather than all the other aspects of a religion—play a major role in religious conflict. Of course, one cannot rule out that there might be such a thing, and it is certainly true that many religious schisms or divisions have been based on theological debates. But it is also noticeable that many things that are called religious conflicts have little to do with any of the theological ideas that may have been responsible for the religious schisms in the first place.

The Yugoslav wars of the 1990s left about 140,000 dead and one million people homeless.

Harris, Hitchens, and Dawkins call these wars religious wars, presumably on the grounds that Serbs tend to be Orthodox Christians, the Croats tend to be Catholics, and many Bosnians are Muslims. But what actually are the differences between these different religions? Let's focus on the difference between the Orthodox Serbs and the Roman Catholic Croats. The Orthodox or Eastern Church split from the Roman Church in 1054, the moment of the Great Schism. Before this they were in communion with one another and the Eastern Church accepted the authority of the pope in Rome. Many complicated conflicts and debates led to this schism, and some of them were genuinely theological. One of the theological issues was the debate over the so-called *filioque* clause. This was a debate about the relative hierarchy of the divinity of the Holy Spirit and Jesus Christ. The traditional view, dating from the Council of Nicaea in 325 and expressed in the so-called Nicene Creed, was that the Holy Spirit "proceeded" from the Father alone. But a later tradition developed that said that the Holy Spirit proceeded from the Father *and* the Son (hence *filioque:* "and the son"). This was eventually adopted by the pope as the revised version of the creed, but it was rejected by the Eastern patriarchs and led to the split between the Roman Catholic Church and the Eastern Orthodox Churches, of which the Serbian Orthodox Church is one.

It would be entirely incorrect, even frivolous, to suggest that the filioque clause is one of the factors that influenced the war between the Serbs and the Croats in the 1990s. And yet, if we are to look at the theological origins of the separation of the Roman and the Orthodox Churches, this would have to be mentioned (among many other details). So if we were going to give an account of the war in terms of "what they believe about God," we would have to mention this. Yet it is plain that this doctrine has nothing more to do with the war than the fact that the Serbs use the Cyrillic alphabet and the Croats use the Latin alphabet.

The known historical facts tell the real story. Yugoslavia was a country created after the First World War, made up of a number of different states with different degrees of dominance and independence. Croatia was a province of the Austro-Hungarian Empire, whereas Serbia had been an independent kingdom since the early nineteenth century. The collapse of the country after President Josip Broz Tito's death in 1980 led to battles for territory and very different conceptions of what belonged to whom; in addition to these "ancient hatreds" and territorial battles, we should also not ignore the role of a collection of ambitious and ruthless individuals. When explaining the beginning of the Serb-Croat conflict, ancient hatreds might play some role; the need for regional dominance plays a role; individual politicians play a role; but what does not play a role is the content of any of the religious doctrines that differ between Catholics and Orthodox. This brief example shows that we should be very careful about giving any role to "beliefs about God" in explaining religious conflict. Many other examples could, I think, show the same thing. The general lesson I want to draw from this brief discussion is how important it is to see religions as a whole, and not simply as collections of theological or cosmological propositions.

The New Atheists might object here that I am parodying their position—as if they were saying that all religious violence is derived from theology alone. Maybe; but they are the ones who treat "religion" as if it were cosmology and theology, and then blame violence on "religion," so conceived. So let's try instead to obtain the outlines of a more realistic picture of religious violence and put theology to one side. I mentioned three further conjectures about the sources of religious violence and conflict: (2) nontheological but distinctively religious aspects of religions; (3) the element of identification; and (4) other nonreligious aspects of human psychology, society, and culture. It is not plausible that each so-called religious conflict can be explained in terms of only one of these; adequate explanations will surely involve them all, to varying degrees. But it might be useful to find examples that illustrate each of these aspects, as a way of separating out the different strands in what is called religious violence or conflict.

By "nontheological but distinctively religious" aspects of religions, I mean things like practices, rituals, structures, and traditions that are essential to the religions themselves but that are not just beliefs about God. The conflict between Shia and Sunni Muslims seems to be an example. This is not a theological struggle, whatever else it is. Sunni Muslims differed from Shias originally in the dispute over who should be the heir of the Prophet Muhammad. One group—who became the Sunnis—followed Abu Bakr, the father of the Prophet's wife. Another group thought that

Ali, Muhammad's cousin and son-in-law, should be his successor. This group became the Shias. This initial succession struggle gave rise to many differences in practice and structure, with Shias placing great importance on the leadership of their imams. About 80 percent of today's Muslims are Sunni, with Indonesia and Saudi Arabia being predominantly Sunni, and Iran the leading Shia nation. The Sunni-Shia conflict has flared up throughout the history of Islam and dominates the current Middle East crisis. Given the religious differences between the two groups, it makes sense to call this a religious conflict, even though it is plain that many other political struggles over power and supremacy in the region are equally important.

It is certainly useful to classify violence as religious when the things people do are explicable by appealing to the content of specific religious doctrines. So, for example, when people are told—by a cleric or a sacred text, say—that they must kill members of another religion simply because they belong to that religion, and not for any further reason, then this is a clear instance of religious violence. Violence based on laws about blasphemy is a good example; the death sentence imposed on the novelist Salman

Rushdie in 1989 by Ayatollah Ruhollah Kho-
meini in Iran is a case in point. In this case, the
violence may be best explained in terms of the
content of some command in a sacred text, or
some interpretation of a religious doctrine. Of
course, other explanations may be offered for
these actions—perhaps political, social, or even
psychoanalytic—but these other explanations do
not eliminate the explanation in terms of religious commitment.

Conjecture (3) is that often what is described
as religious conflict comes from something that
is an essential part of religion but is also found
elsewhere: the element of identification. People
deeply identify with their nation or particular social group, fighting, often to the death, against
those who are perceived to be dominating them
or oppressing them. Another example discussed
by Dawkins and Hitchens, Northern Ireland,
seems to be of this kind.

The Northern Ireland conflict was at its height
in the last few decades of the twentieth century,
though its roots go back a few hundred years. In
the seventeenth century there were violent conflicts in the north of Ireland between Protestant
settlers from England and Scotland and the Irish
Catholic population. The Protestants were sup-

ported by the English government and its army, and this culminated in the violent conquest of the whole of Ireland by Oliver Cromwell and his soldiers. When Irish independence from Britain was established in 1922, the island was divided, with the northern section (Ulster, inhabited by a Protestant majority) remaining part of what became the United Kingdom. In the 1960s conflict flared up again, the immediate cause being a civil rights campaign against anti-Catholic discrimination, and continued until the end of the century.

Although it is often described as conflict between Catholics and Protestants, the details of religious belief have played almost no role in the Northern Ireland conflict. Whatever the doctrinal differences between Catholics and Protestants actually are, it was not these things that provoked the conflict but specific historical events relating to the treatment of the Ulster Catholic minority, against the background of massive resentment. Hitchens reports a familiar joke from the Northern Irish conflict:

A man is stopped at a roadblock and asked his religion. When he replies that he is an atheist he is asked, "Protestant or Catholic atheist?" I think this shows how the obsession has rotted even the legendary local sense of humour.[11]

Hitchens misses the point here—far from rotting the local sense of humor, the joke is a nice example of it. For what the joke shows is not that religion is the immovable force in the conflict but that actual belief in God is irrelevant. What matters is what group you belong to. Of course, the groups are identified by the names of the religions they belong to, but (to state what should have been obvious to Hitchens) what the joke illustrates is that the religious content of the doctrines associated with these names is not significant.

At the heart of the Northern Irish conflict was the struggle of one group that felt itself to be oppressed by another, and many members of the former group hoped for unity with another nation. In some ways it resembles other twentieth-century struggles for political independence—in Europe, the Basque region and Catalonia are similar in the first respect—in that it involves identification as a driving force in the struggle. Religion plays some role in the Northern Irish conflict, but in this case only because religion is the locus of identification. My suggestion is that we can call the Northern Irish conflict a "religious conflict" if we like—though few do, outside New Atheist circles—but only so long as we bear in mind that its driving force is something that we find in other regional conflicts too: identification.

In short, one thing that drives groups of people to kill, fight, and harass each other is the complex relationship of identification that people have to their social groups. Identification is independent of religion, in the sense that it can exist without religion—but, as I argued in Chapter 3, it is an element in religion. This is why some people find it so natural to call some conflicts religious, though others may want to call them "ethnic." As we saw previously, Dawkins thinks that the "ethnic" in the phrase "ethnic cleansing" is a "euphemism for religious cleansing."[12] What does "ethnic" really mean in this context? Ethnicity is not about a genetic or biological feature of people—there are no such features that identify all people of the same ethnicity. But this does not mean ethnicity is not real. An ethnicity is, for the most part, a shared language, a shared religion, a shared believed history of a group, or some combination of these. Dawkins is right, then, that there is a connection between the idea of ethnic cleansing and religion; but that is only because religion is one of the marks of ethnicity. Since shared religion can be part of the underlying reality of ethnicity, it is not a euphemism to call religious disputes "ethnic"—it can just be another way of picking out the same fact.

The fourth factor in explaining religious violence or conflict is what I called other nonreligious aspects of human psychology, society, and culture. Violence may be motivated by revenge, or by a sense of hopelessness—the "no future" view of life reported by some studies of European jihadists. There is evidence that some of those who join IS and other groups do so because they feel that there is nothing to live for, and they find meaning in the strong bonds and uncompromising message of violent jihadism. Other recent religious terrorists belong to the so-called lone wolf category—men who pursue their goal of a kind of fame and immortality through the notoriety of mass murder—here having more in common with the phenomenon of school shooters in the United States or mass murderers like Timothy McVeigh and Anders Breivik than with other religious warriors.

The complexity of factors that move people toward religious violence, it seems to me, defies any serious attempt to characterize religion as uniquely bad in the way that the New Atheists do. But one lesson we can draw at this point is that even when a conflict is typically—and correctly—described in religious terms, this does not by itself mean that religion is the driving force in that conflict. This is true of the examples discussed previously—Yugoslavia and Northern Ireland—and it seems to me to be true also of one of the deadliest of the European "wars of religion," the Thirty Years' War.

This war is often taken to be the paradigm of a religious conflict, a result of the previous century's Reformation and the splitting of Europe between the Catholic and Protestant faiths. On one side there was the (Catholic) Habsburg Holy Roman Emperor, with his allies in Spain and other Catholic countries. On the other side there were the Bohemian Protestants and the northern European Protestant countries: Sweden, some of the German states, Denmark, and the Dutch Republic. The war started because of disagreements among the smaller states of the empire about their freedom of religion, and its origins are clearly traceable to the fragile peace declared at the end of the sixteenth century's Wars of Religion. As the conflict grew from central Europe to the north and to the west, France entered the war on the side of the Protestant countries. Someone might argue that the fact that Catholic France fought on the side of the Protestant countries shows that the war was not really a religious conflict. But there was also, nonetheless, an undeniable religious element of the second kind I identified previously. Historians agree that among the causes of the war were disputes between Protestants and Catholics about the freedom to practice their faith; Protestants in Bohemia felt threatened by the fanatical new emperor, and their churches were destroyed. However, the fact that this terrible conflict ended with a number of powerful Catholic countries fighting one another does underline the importance of taking into account factors other than religion.

Those who want to blame religion for the violence of the world may continue to insist that religion was the most *fundamental* component in (say) the Thirty Years' War. But given the complexity of the political and other motivations behind the major actors in a tragedy like this, what is the point of declaring these events to be "fundamentally" religious? The historical evidence points in favor of many complex motives in the pursuit of power and hegemony in Europe in the seventeenth century. Religion is one factor, without doubt. But is it the most fundamental or important factor? How can we go about answering this question? Is there even any need to answer it? If you have the New Atheists' view of religion as something uniquely bad, then I can see why you might want to answer the question. But how can you have this assumption without having first assessed the evidence? Better to settle for a plain, factual, empirical assessment of the many causes and factors that led to complex conflicts like this.

What should we conclude about religious violence? We should reject the extreme view that the worst violence in human history has been religious, and the equally implausible view that there is really no such thing as religious violence. The real question is what it means for violence to be religious, and what it is about religion that gives rise to violence, often of an extreme form. The extreme violence in these cases is often explicable in terms of the tendency of identification (religious or not) to exclude and discriminate against others; the violent content of some religious texts; or the struggle for power, supremacy, or autonomy among competing religious groups—in addition to human motivations and desires (for example, for revenge) that are intelligible independently of anything to do with religion.

IRRATIONALITY

I suspect that what lies behind the New Atheists' arguments about religious violence is captured by the slogan, "those who can make you believe absurdities can make you commit atrocities"—the common translation of a remark of Voltaire's.[13] The New Atheists' case against religion often involves the claim that there is some connection between the absurdity of religious beliefs and the terrible things that religions make believers do. The connection is often made through the idea of irrationality. It is because religious beliefs are so deeply irrational that believers are led to believe things that are absurd, and, therefore, as Voltaire's remark suggests, they are then up for anything. For some writers, this is what authoritarian nonreligious regimes and religions really have in common. Here is Harris on the communist regime in North Korea, for example, defending his idea that even communism is a kind of religion:

While our differences with North Korea, for instance, are not explicitly religious, they are a direct consequence of the North Koreans' having grown utterly deranged by their political ideology, their abject worship of their leaders. . . . The problem of North Korea is, first and foremost, a problem of the unjustified (and unjustifiable) beliefs of North Koreans.[14]

What is supposed to be wrong with both religion and the communist regimes, then, is that they have unjustified beliefs: they are irrational. In the spirit of Voltaire's remark, Harris links this irrationality with the wickedness that religion can bring about:

Whenever a man imagines that he need only believe the truth of a proposition, without evidence—that unbelievers will go to hell, that Jews drink the blood of infants—he becomes capable of anything.[15]

The idea that religious belief is a pervasive form of irrationality deriving from something deep in the human psyche, a kind of pathology of the mind, is one that has been common since the Enlightenment, and it also finds expression in both Marxian and Freudian critiques of religion. Karl Marx's image of religion as the opium of the people presents its effects as those of intoxication—though opium can, of course, give relief from real pain and suffering. Sigmund Freud's idea of an infantile delusion similarly places the nature of religious belief outside rational control. Understandably, the religious are unable to accept this description of their system of thought. We encounter again the familiar consequence that the atheists are unable to make sense of their disagreement with their opponents.

While there certainly are insights contained within the Marxian and Freudian views, their large-scale visions are surely implausible and we should reject them. What I would rather focus on here is the question of irrationality itself: What does it mean, in general, to be rational or irrational, and to what extent do religious beliefs fail the tests for rationality?

Philosophers distinguish between theoretical rationality—what it is reasonable or rational to believe—and practical rationality—what it is reasonable or rational to do. Thus both beliefs and actions can be assessed as rational or irrational. What theoretical and practical rationality have in common is the notion of a reason: for a belief to be rational is for it to be based on reasons; likewise for action. What is a reason? The most concise and general definition, in my view, was given by T. M. Scanlon: a reason for something is a "consideration that counts in favour of it."[16] So a reason for believing something is a consideration that counts in favor of believing it, and a reason for doing something is a consideration that counts in favor of doing it.

Since this book is about religious belief, I will concentrate mostly on theoretical rationality, or reasons for belief. A belief is rational when there are some reasons in its favor—but it is natural to add that the reasons must be *good* ones. Some philosophers, however, talk about "having a reason" in a way that implies that there cannot really be bad reasons. On this view, if a reason is a consideration that counts in favor of doing or thinking something, then what we might ordinarily call a "bad reason" is better construed as something that someone *thinks* is a reason but is not really one. A gambler might think, for example, that the fact that the color red has come up on the roulette wheel the last thirty times is a reason for believing that black will come up next. But as any student of chance will know, this is not the case. Does this mean the gambler has a bad reason for believing something, or no reason at all?

For my purposes here, it doesn't matter how we answer this question. It matters for other questions in the philosophy of reasons and rationality, but not for the question of the rationality of religious belief. So I will continue to talk in the ordinary way about people having good or bad reasons for believing or thinking things. I will say that someone's reason for believing something, in this ordinary sense, is a consideration that they *think* counts in favor of it—but they may be wrong. One way in which someone might be irrational, then, is when one believes something but one's reasons are not good enough.

What can we say, in general, about what it is for reasons to be good reasons for belief? Sometimes it is said—as Harris does in the quote provided earlier—that one should only believe something on the basis of evidence, but this just raises a new question: What is evidence? Again, different views have been offered of what evidence is, with many thinkers arguing that evidence must come from the believer's own sensory experiences—this was the view expressed by Saint Thomas the Apostle when he said that he would not believe that Jesus is risen until he could put his hands in the hole in his side, and his fingers in the holes in his hands. But in other kinds of cases we do not rely on the evidence of our senses alone: much of what we learn relies on the testimony of others, for example. The fact that a reliable person told me something can be a good reason for believing it, even if I have no immediate sensory or perceptual knowledge of what they are talking about. Additionally, much scientific reasoning is based on mathematics, and the reasons for believing mathematical truths are not sensory either (it's not a good answer to the question, "Why is the Pythagorean theorem true?" to say, "I can just see it!").

I will say that someone can have a reason for believing something even if this belief is, in fact, not true. Pre-Copernican astronomers had reasons to believe the sun orbited the earth, we can assume—they were not irrational fools—but nonetheless this belief was false. So if a *justified* belief is one for which there is a reason, this is compatible with its being a false belief. The important interim conclusion, then, is that a belief can be false—that is, untrue, incorrect—without being irrational. Someone can do their best by the lights of current knowledge and evidence and yet end up with a false belief.

Anyway, if these are some of the various features of good reasons for belief, then a *bad* reason for believing something would be one that was, for example, in conflict with sensory evidence, or with the best testimony, or with the kind of reasons offered in mathematics. In what way might a religious belief be irrational in this sense—that is, based on wholly bad or inadequate reasons?

Clearly, there might be many ways. Consider my description from Chapter 2 of the core content of religious belief, as described by William James: "the belief that there is an unseen order, and that our supreme good lies in harmoniously adjusting ourselves to it." Someone might believe that there is an unseen order because they want to believe it; because it makes them seem deep or clever; because someone they admired told them so, despite that person's manifest irresponsibility about matters of fact; or because they have been indoctrinated in some way into believing it. I'm sure we can all think of familiar cases like these: as with many beliefs, religious beliefs can be held for bad reasons, even for obviously bad reasons—and in that sense they can be held irrationally.

But must this be so? Is it *necessary* that someone who believes that there is an unseen order believe it for bad reasons? If the religious belief *itself* is irrational by its very nature, then it would seem that it could not be held for good reasons. But is this true? It doesn't seem so. Someone could believe that there is an unseen order because they have carefully considered all the arguments for the opposite and have found them wanting; or because they have found some phenomena that they have very good reasons to believe are not accounted for except through the idea of an unseen order.

The fact that someone believes something for a good reason (in this sense) is consistent with the belief's being false. So if you agree with me, as an atheist, that there is no unseen order, then you may also question believers' reasons for believing in this. But the issue I am looking at here is not whether any reasons for believing in the unseen order are ones I would accept—that is, whether the religious belief is true. The issue is whether such a belief must be irrational. If we assume that this means *always based on bad reasons,* then the answer seems to be no.

However, maybe this assumption is too strong and makes it too easy for me to get to the conclusion that religious belief is not irrational. Maybe a type of belief's being irrational is not that it *must* be based on bad reasons, but merely that it generally is. Might religious beliefs be like this? In other words, might it just be a fact that most of the time, religious beliefs are based on bad reasons, even if there might be some occasional good reasons for such beliefs. Whether this is true is not something that can be established by a philosophical investigation like the current one—it needs empirical investigation into the actual psychology of believers, a massive and difficult task. But even if it were true, it would not touch my claim that religious belief is not *necessarily* irrational.

Another possible objection here is that religious belief need not be founded on reasons at all. This idea may be appealed to by the religious—in defense of the idea that religious belief is a matter of faith alone—and by their critics—as an attempt to show how the minds of the believers can be corrupted (for example) by the emotional appeal of charismatic preachers or demagogues.

There is clearly some truth in this latter point, and so I need to tread more carefully when stating exactly what the relation is between religious belief and reason. The most I think I can insist on here is that religious belief is not necessarily irrational, that there can be considerations that people take to count in its favor, and that these people need not be unreasonable in doing so. But it obviously happens also that the religious can be swept away by passions that eliminate any appeal to reason, and that this can have bad psychological and social effects, some of which I have described earlier in this chapter. It is just that this need not be the case—such things do not follow from the very essence of religion as I see it.

I've been talking here about how reasons bear on the rationality of a belief. Another way in which someone can be irrational relates not to their *reasons*—things that count in favor of believing—but to their *reasoning:* that is, to the processes that lead them to their beliefs. Theories of rationality specify not just what it is for something to be a reason but also what it is for someone *to reason*. Different styles of reasoning are distinguished, but one general abstract structure is common to those styles. In this structure a thinker moves from a collection of beliefs or assumptions or suppositions that they already have and draws a conclusion from them. This collection of beliefs and so on can be called the *premises* of the reasoning. Good reasoning, then, is about good ways of getting from the premises one already has to new conclusions.

What is a "good" way of getting from premises to conclusions? This question is addressed, in different ways, by logic and other theories of reasoning. In one kind of good reasoning, the truth of the premises guarantees the truth of the conclusion—if you start from truths, you can only move to other truths in your conclusions. In another, the premises support the conclusion as evidence. Bad reasoning may involve fallacies—taking a conclusion to be guaranteed or supported by premises when in fact it is not. And some connections between thoughts or ideas are not reasoning at all. For example, the mere association between one idea and another—something just "popping into your mind"—does not really count as reasoning at all.

An important aspect of theories of reasoning or rationality is that they typically do not say anything about what sorts of things a rational person should believe; they do not put restrictions on what sorts of "contents" our beliefs should have, to use the terminology introduced in Chapter 1. They only specify what it is for something to be a reason, or what it is to be a process of good reasoning. In other words, a theory of rationality is not a device you can use to *tell you what to believe.* It will only tell you (at best) what processes you should use to get from what you already believe to other beliefs. So it is hard to see how any theory of rationality (in this specific sense) can legislate on whether religious belief, as such, is rational.

Given all this, what should we conclude about the rationality of religious belief in general? We need to recognize that a belief's being false is not necessarily the same as its being irrational. Whether a belief is rational or irrational depends on the quality of the reasons on which it is based, the quality of the reasoning that led to it, or both. To assess whether any given religious belief is irrational we need to assess these two things. Many people may hold religious beliefs for bad reasons, to be sure; but there may also be good reasons for believing these things. People may be led to false belief through bad reasoning or through no reasoning at all; but there are also cases in which people are led to such beliefs through reasoning that is not so bad. To show that religious belief is, as such, irrational, you would need to show that it can never be based on good reasoning or on good reasons. I don't think this can be done. So I resist the idea that religious belief as such is irrational. Many or most religious beliefs are not true, but that is not the same thing.

What should we say, then, about those agnostics who still keep the flame of hope alive, or flickering in their soul, and may even pray on occasion? Are they irrational? Anthony Kenny said the right thing about this, it seems to me:

Some find something comic in the idea of an agnostic praying to a God whose existence he doubts. It is surely no more unreasonable than the act of a man adrift in the ocean, trapped in a cave, or stranded on a mountainside, who cries for help though he may never be heard or fires a signal which may never be seen.[17]

As we have seen, rationality matters for some of the New Atheist thinkers because they think that there is some connection between people's failures of rationality and the wicked things they do. This connection might be supposed to be because of some necessary connection between irrationality itself and evil, as Harris suggests; or it might be a psychological generalization about human beings (that irrational people are more wicked than rational people). Both ideas are very problematic. The idea that there is some kind of connection between reason and morality is one that is familiar from the philosophy of Immanuel Kant. Kant thought that if we properly grasped what rationality or reason demands from us, it would reveal our moral obligations to one another. But Kant's views do not imply that every failing in rationality will lead to some moral failing—only that the ultimate basis for what he called the "moral law" is reason.

And as a generalization about human psychology, the idea that there is a correlation between irrationality and wickedness is very implausible. The obvious facts are that reasonable, rational, educated, and knowledgeable people can be wicked and vicious; ignorant, irrational people can be good and kind. And vice versa. It seems to me that behind the New Atheists' passion lies a certain optimism about human nature: that with religion eliminated, we will see the world aright and will become better people. A glance at recent human history shows how questionable this connection is. There is little evidence that people would be any better if religion were to wither away: remember once again the atrocities of the twentieth century and how little they owe to religion. A broader historical view should help put the more excitable claims of the New Atheists in perspective.

My picture of religion in this book has been drawn from a great distance and is, of course, idealized in certain respects. I do not mean to imply that religious believers are all motivated by the pure and explicit recognition of what I am calling the religious impulse; nor do I deny that religious people can be as prejudiced, blinkered, exclusive, and simple-minded as any human being. And it should be obvious from this chapter, I hope, that the role of religion in the history of documented human conflict does not cast the world's great faiths in a very positive light.

But nonetheless I maintain that any external assessment of the value of religion as a whole has to take into account its enormous positive value in many people's lives. By this I don't just mean the comfort that can come from mistaken beliefs about (say) life after death—something that is not, in any case, necessary to all believers in the monotheistic religions, let alone in all religions. I mean, more importantly, the sense of belonging to a culture and having a history; the sense of the ineffable in the world; the sense that there is value in something beyond the satisfaction of one's desires of the present moment. Some of these things can be had without religion; but religion crystallizes them for so many people to provide a sense of who they are. In addition, it is not wise for us simply to ignore the value of our history, or the undeniable fact that even many atheist ideas have been formed by Christianity. Some recent writers (Gray, for example) regard this as a criticism of atheism; I do not.

In this chapter I have addressed those atheists who take religion as the main source of the world's problems, or the problems of the world as deriving from religion, and who see the problems of religion as deriving from cosmological belief. A popular New Atheist assumption is that we can therefore point out the errors in these cosmological beliefs and thus help solve the problems of the world by a process of rational belief change. But even if religious belief were in some straightforward way the source of the main problems of the world—which I doubt, for the reasons given here—it is not obvious that the best way to deal with this is to try to change people's beliefs by telling them that they are stupid, irrational, or hopelessly ignorant. How then should atheists confront or otherwise deal with those with whom they do not agree? Chapter 5 will address this question.

5

The Meaning of Tolerance

THE INESCAPABILITY OF RELIGION

In the days of the Cold War, there was a popular way of making sense of human society as a whole and the structure of its conflicts. The central question, which dominated disputes about the difference between East and West, and the difference between Left and Right, was the role of the state in industrialized societies. How much should the state own or control? What restrictions should there be on private ownership and trade? How much should the state plan its economy, and to what extent is this possible? The Soviet model provided one kind of answer ("a lot") and the United States and Western Europe provided another kind of answer (ranging from "as little as possible, apart from certain essential facilities and utilities," to "quite a lot"). Some thinkers saw this conflict as explained in terms of Marxist ideas about capital and labor; others believed the conflict would be resolved in the inexorable triumph of the Western liberal ideas of freedom and democracy.

These days things look very different. With the total collapse of the Soviet model in the late 1980s and the growth of capitalism even in one vast country that is still nominally communist (China), the question of the role and limits of state ownership does not provide us with the clear divisions it used to. In fact, the old question seems less and less fundamental to understanding either how human societies function or how they should. The old question obscured what is now clearer: that the main drivers behind world events are religion and nationhood, not principles about state ownership and the economy.

As I said at the beginning of this book, of the world's 7.1 billion people, about 6 billion identify as belonging to some religion or other. Three of the world's four most populous countries—

India, the United States, and Indonesia—have huge religious populations. China, with the largest population in the world, might seem an exception. But in China too, religion is growing at a striking rate. A 2006 survey showed that 31 percent of Chinese people regard religion as somewhat important in their lives, and only 11 percent now express the communist view that it is not important. In 2010, the Pew Research Center estimated that there are sixty-seven million practicing Christians in China; a small proportion of the vast Chinese population but a huge number of people nonetheless—more than the current population of the United Kingdom—and, as the product of the last few decades of slow social liberalization in China, it can be expected to increase.[1]

Some New Atheists have claimed that religion is in decline worldwide, but this strikes me as wishful thinking. There is no serious prospect that the religious impulse and religious structures will disappear from human societies. Given this, it seems that the urgent question facing those of us who reject religious belief is how we should accommodate religion. The question divides into two—there is the practical, personal, or moral question of how atheists should accommodate religion and believers in their own lives and in their own personal view of the world, and there is the political question of how secular states should make room for religious believers. The political question is too large a task for this book; I will concentrate on the first, the personal question.

As I observed at the beginning of this book, the contemporary debate about religious belief is fraught and combative. New Atheists present a picture of religious belief and practice as a worthless enterprise based on premodern cosmology, superstition, and irrational prejudice. Believers respond by arguing that atheists miss the point, that they misunderstand the nature of belief, or that they display the same "fundamentalist" tendencies that they criticize in some believers.

Many atheists are combative precisely because they see this difference of worldviews as a real conflict in need of urgent solutions. They see religion as causing huge problems in the world: violence, repression of action and thought, and the attempt to interfere with proper education and intellectual progress. This is why they think religion needs to be tackled and cannot simply be tolerated. Their practical attitude to religious belief is to attempt to use rational argument and scientific evidence to combat its bad effects, to enable those whom they see to be entrapped by it to escape it, and perhaps, in some ideal future, to eliminate it entirely.

No one should object to attempts to combat the bad effects of religious belief: the intolerance, the violence, and the restriction on freedom of thought and action that some religious groups and institutions unquestionably promote. The question is, rather, how should we fit these specific objections to the actions of the religious into a general attitude to religion as a whole? Do we think of what is wrong with these things as stemming from very general objections to religious belief *as such* that we must roll out whenever we can, in the hope of working toward the elimination of as much of it as possible? Or should we think instead of these things as having many different explanations, some of which are essentially connected to religion and some of which are not, and acknowledge that a blanket critique based on a general opposition to "religion" is not likely to be explanatory or effective?

My view, of course, is the latter. In Chapter 4 I criticized the idea that there is, in general, one clear and isolatable "religious" component to many of the things that have counted as religious conflicts over the centuries. Religious conflict can have religious motivations; it can have non-religious motivations; and sometimes these are inextricably mixed. It is not the case that religion has been responsible for the worst atrocities in human history, but in various complex ways it has been responsible for a lot of misery.

The New Atheist critique of religion is based on the largely cosmological picture of the content of religious belief that I criticized in Chapter 2. If this is your picture of religious belief, then this may be why you think that undermining this cosmology is a way to criticize those who promote violence for religious ends or for religious reasons. But not only is it incredibly unlikely that a critique of a cosmology will have any effect on addressing these problems; it is also unclear what cosmology has to do with them anyway, for the reasons I gave in Chapter 4.

My account of religion does better. The phenomenon of identification in terms of which I describe religious belief can be used to explain some kinds of religious violence, as I explained in Chapter 4. Moreover, the fact that identification occurs outside religious contexts makes the violence that is a result of religious identification more intelligible, since it can be seen as part of a more general pattern in human societies and human history.

I agree with John Gray, then, when he says that "the most necessary task of the present time is to accept the irreducible reality of religion."[2] Religion is a deep, pervasive, and probably ineliminable aspect of human society, with some good features and some bad. The attitude I want to extract from these reflections has two sides: an attempt at understanding, and an attempt at tolerance. Understanding, because we should try to understand that which we reject, as well as that which we accept. Tolerance, because our aim should not be to covert those with whom we disagree but rather to live in peace with them. What we are after, in Gray's words, is "a type of toleration whose goal is not truth but peace."[3]

RELATIVISM AND RESPECT

What does it mean, then, to tolerate religion in one's life? In his book *Why Tolerate Religion?,* the philosopher Brian Leiter argues that religion can make no special claim on a state for toleration. Leiter's conclusions are plausible, but of limited interest, restricted as they are to the context of legislation in contemporary American society.[4]

Most of our personal interactions with one another are not legal in character—thank God, I
want to say—so concentration on the law gives
us little guidance about the role and nature of
toleration outside these contexts. As David Lewis
nicely put it,

> Legal rights are far from the whole story. The insti-
> tutions of toleration are in large part informal, a
> matter not of law but of custom, habits of conduct
> and thought. Even when the law lets us do as we like,
> many of us do not like to do anything that would
> make people suffer for the opinions they hold, or
> hinder their expression of their opinions.[5]

We need to investigate the nature of these cus-
toms and habits independently of the question of
what the law should say. This is what I will begin
to do here.

I begin with some familiar atheist criticisms
of religious tolerance. The idea that atheists
should tolerate religion—and that religions should
tolerate one other—is frequently criticized for
two reasons: first, because it implies a kind of
relativism, an "anything goes" approach to
belief and truth; and second, because it implies
a wishy-washy "respect" for religious beliefs.

Both criticisms are misguided: tolerance implies neither relativism nor respect for the beliefs of others.

Let's take relativism first. Relativism is the view that truth is relative to a worldview or a standpoint. It says that the same claim can be true from one standpoint but not true from another. For example, relativism implies that the claim that *eating meat is always wrong* is true from the standpoint of a committed vegetarian, but the very same claim is not true from the standpoint of a committed carnivore. So claims are not true or false as such—if you say that a claim is true, you always need to answer the question, true for whom?

Some people take the fact of disagreement as a reason for believing in relativism. For example, the fact that the vegetarian and the carnivore will never agree is supposed to be a reason for thinking that, in their own way, each of them is right: the vegetarian is right from his standpoint and the carnivore is right from hers. How is this argument supposed to work? How do we get from disagreement to relative truth?

We can't. The mere fact of disagreement does not mean that all truth is relative. If you and I disagree about the date on which Archduke

Franz Ferdinand was assassinated—suppose you think it was in June 1914 and I think it was in August 1914—this does not mean that its being in August is true for me and its being in June is true for you. In this case we can easily determine who is right and who is wrong. But what if we cannot determine this? If a dispute cannot be settled by the appeal to facts, does this imply relativism about the subject matter of that dispute? Again, the answer is, obviously not. It may be impossible to assess whether some ordinary factual claim today is true—say, that I had over one hundred thousand hairs on my head ten years ago—but this does not mean there is no fact of the matter about how many hairs I had on my head then. There was such a fact; it is just one of the many that is lost in the dustbin of history. Whether anyone can show today whether it is true is not relevant.

It could be said that these objections are not to the point, since—as the example of vegetarianism shows—relativism is only really plausible in the moral sphere. It is in connection with moral beliefs that we often find irreconcilable disagreements, and it is not so obvious here that there is such a thing as a "fact of the matter" that will decide things one way or another. Which fact or facts, for example, could settle the question of whether the moral vegetarian is right or wrong? For some people, the obscurity about what this kind of "fact" might be leads to the conclusion that because there is nothing that could settle a moral dispute, there cannot be any objective moral truths or facts.

However, it's not so clear how this is connected to relativism, since relativism is not the view that there are *no* moral facts or truths. That kind of view has had various names in philosophy—nihilism, skepticism, nonfactualism, irrealism—but relativism is not one of them. Relativism is the view that truth (whether moral or not) is relative, not that truth does not exist. So it's not clear how appealing to the obscurity of the idea of a moral fact will help the case for relativism. It might seem as if there is a connection—"If nothing can possibly establish whether A or B is right about some subject matter, then truth must be relative to A's and B's perspective"—but this connection crumbles under the slightest scrutiny.

And so does relativism. For the underlying problem with relativism about truth is that it cannot be coherently stated by someone who believes it. If *all* truth is relative, then in what sense is relativism itself true? It can't be true in any absolute, objective sense, since nothing is true in this sense. So it must be true in the only sense that relativism itself allows: true relative to some framework or standpoint. But if relativism itself is only relatively true, then it does not command the assent of those of us who are not relativists. By relativism's own lights, it is true for relativists but not true for nonrelativists. So it looks like we can ignore it.

Relativism about truth, then, seems a nonstarter. But one curious feature of philosophical discussions of relativism is that those who defend relativism frequently take it to be obviously true, and those who attack it take it to be obviously false, perhaps for the reasons we have just discussed. This suggests that those debating this issue may have different ideas in mind even when using the same words (as W. V. Quine once put it, "Assertions startlingly false on the face of them often turn on hidden differences of language"[6]). And this is sometimes how it is with relativism. For taken at face value, relativism does imply obvious falsehoods. It would seem to imply that "The sun orbits the earth" is true relative to the pre-Copernican worldview but false according to ours. If we then add that neither of these worldviews is absolutely correct or incorrect, but only relatively so, then it was not incorrect according to the pre-Copernicans to say that the sun orbits the earth. But if this is so, then Copernicus did not show that the astronomers before him were wrong, since they weren't wrong. But this is absurd. If Copernicus did anything at all, he showed that these astronomers were wrong.

Or is it so absurd? What if we mean by "true according to their worldview" simply that *it is part of their worldview?* In other words, we just mean that they *think* it's true—and this doesn't mean that it really is true. For their worldview might be incorrect. So "true according to X's worldview" just means that it is *what X believes or thinks.* That's all. That doesn't mean that truth itself is different according to different worldviews, only that people with different worldviews hold different things to be true. This is, obviously enough, part of what it is to be a worldview: a collection of beliefs. And we can say the same about something's being "true for me" but not "true for you": it just means that I hold the view to be true but you don't. This is consistent with one of us being right and the other being wrong.

If this is what we mean by relativism, though, it has very little to do with the idea of truth. It is rather a view about belief and disagreement: the unexceptionable view that people have different beliefs about the world, some of these beliefs conflict, and that having a belief is holding something to be true. This clearly does not imply that truth *itself* is relative in any other way. The truth is just what it is.

Another thing that might be meant by relativism is the view that we should be cautious and not too dogmatic when making claims to knowledge. We should be aware that our views in the past have turned out to be wrong, and so we should be cautious about affirming our current views too dogmatically. We need to leave open the possibility that we might be wrong. But once again, this does not imply a relative view of truth itself. Being wrong is a matter of discovering that we are not right—in other words, that what we believe is not true. So this attitude seems to presuppose the idea of an absolute truth, rather than undermine it.

These are some of the things that could be meant by relativism, then: there are different worldviews; and we should be cautious and not dogmatic. But these ideas are not the same as the idea that *truth itself* is relative. This idea—that how things are, the facts, the way reality is, and so on are somehow dependent on our perspective or worldview, and that since different worldviews differ, the truth differs— cannot really be made coherent. But if relativism is incoherent, then it is good that the doctrine of toleration does not imply it—I want to defend the doctrine of toleration, and it would not be good for me if it implied something inco- herent. Fortunately this is not the case. But it is worth dwelling briefly on what the connection between toleration and relativism is supposed to be.

Toleration might be thought to imply rela- tivism either because toleration involves an acknowledgment that we *cannot* always change people's beliefs, or because toleration implies that we have no *right* to try to change people's beliefs. However, the first claim is a non sequitur, and the second has nothing to do with toleration, properly understood. The first claim is a non se- quitur because it is simply a fact that we cannot always change people's beliefs—this is a claim about people, not about truth. It is perfectly con- sistent with the idea that the truth is absolute and objective and "out there." Having these nonrelativist views of truth does not imply anything about whether we can persuade others—that depends on their individual psychologies and our powers of persuasion, among other things.

The claim that we have no "right" to change someone else's belief has, in itself, nothing to do with toleration. Indeed, toleration is quite consistent with the idea that we have every right to change the beliefs of others when (for example) they are incorrect. The very institution of education underlines this: What is education, after all, but the systematic attempt to change and, ideally, improve the beliefs of others?

But, it might be said, doesn't the toleration of a view imply at least that we do not disapprove of it? This idea is actually quite widespread in public debate, but it is not true. In fact, as a number of philosophers have pointed out, it is the opposite of the truth. Susan Mendus puts it neatly: "One necessary condition of toleration is the presence of disapproval or hostility."[7] So toleration of something *implies* disapproval of it: you can only tolerate those things of which you disapprove or submit to some other kind of negative assessment. I don't *tolerate* those things I like—good music or good food, for example—

or those things to which I am indifferent. But I may tolerate my neighbors' unpleasant, loud music and the smelly food they cook at their parties. I may do this because, for example, they told me in advance about the party, they do not complain about my own noise, we are generally on good terms, and I want to be on good terms with those who live around me and to avoid unnecessary conflict. So I tolerate it. Nonetheless, I dislike their music and their smelly food, and in an ideal world I might prefer it if I did not have to experience this.

This point brings us to the second common objection to the toleration of religious belief: that tolerance implies respect for views that do not deserve respect. Like the idea that tolerance implies relativism, the objection is confused and needs to be picked apart.

Of course, there is nothing mistaken or contradictory in an atheist respecting aspects of a religious tradition or religious beliefs. Atheists might respect or even admire the great art or music or architecture that Christianity has produced, or the idea of self-sacrifice, or some moral ideals—for example, the ideal of endless compassion, or that expressed in "He who is without sin, cast the first stone." But atheists are not obliged to respect religious beliefs just because they tolerate them. On the contrary, as I have just pointed out, tolerance of something implies that one objects to, disapproves of, or has some other negative assessment of it. We do not tolerate views that we think are basically OK or reasonable even if we do not share them. Toleration is not indifference.

So tolerating the religious is not a matter of saying that their views are equally worthy of respect. Nor is it a matter of saying they are "entitled to their own opinion." If your opinions are vile and bigoted—if you believe that adulterers should be stoned, or that doctors who perform abortions should be killed—then you are not entitled to these opinions, they are not worthy of anyone's respect. The idea that all views or opinions are worthy of respect is entirely false.

What is closer to the truth, however, is that all *people,* rather than their opinions, are worthy of respect. This is one way to express the ideal in liberal societies that each person in a certain sense counts for one and no one counts for more than one—an ideal expressed in the democratic practice of one person, one vote. It is also related to the idea that liberal societies are "societies of equals." (And it is connected, obviously enough, to the Christian idea that God loves us all equally.)

Whatever exactly this means, it cannot mean that each person receives exactly the same moral evaluation—some people are wicked and some are good, so equal respect for persons cannot mean they all get the same score. Nor can it mean that each person's life is equally worthwhile—that is, that any person's actual life contains as much of value as any other's. This can't be true—many people's lives are sad and miserable, devoid of pleasure, happiness, and satisfaction. Other lives are enriched by love and friendship, good fortune, achievement, and other things that bring contentment. Being worthy of respect is not a statement about the quality of people's lives but rather a statement about how people should be treated: as autonomous agents, equal before morality and the law. As Immanuel Kant put it in one of his most profound insights, morality requires that people be treated not as means to further ends but as ends in themselves. And we can respect people in this sense without respecting their views.

I have been arguing that tolerance does not require respect for the views one is tolerating. But it does go hand in hand with respect for people as autonomous individuals in this broadly Kantian sense. Some writers disagree. Tariq Ramadan, for example, seems to think that tolerance is *opposed* to respect for others. Ramadan has argued that "when it comes to relations between free and equal human beings, autonomous and independent nations, or civilizations, religions and cultures, appeals for the tolerance of others are no longer relevant." This is because "when we are on equal terms, it is no longer a matter of conceding tolerance, but of rising above that and educating ourselves to respect others."[8] But why should we think that when we learn to respect others then we do not need to tolerate them? One answer, suggested by Frank Furedi, is that Ramadan thinks that tolerance is really a form of paternalism, and that once we move away from such a morally patronizing position to the true relativistic position, then we will see it for what it is.[9]

But tolerance is not paternalism, since paternalism implies that one should intervene in people's lives for their own best interests, whereas tolerance involves living together, with conflicting views, without always intervening. And it is puzzling why it should be morally patronizing to hold a view, to think your opponent is

THE MEANING OF BELIEF

wrong, and yet not attempt to change your opponent's belief or regulate their behaviour.

Moreover, Ramadan's view ignores the distinction between respecting views and respecting people, which I think is the only way to make sense of a general appeal to the idea of "respect." And respecting people is entirely compatible with thinking their views are wrong, confused, irrational, or wicked. Respect in this sense would imply, for example, that those who act on their wrong or wicked views should still be treated as autonomous human beings who have responsibility for their actions. When implemented in law or a political system, respect manifests itself in the equality of all citizens before the law, freedom from arbitrary interference, and the right to vote, among other things.

Tolerance, then, is not about respecting the sensitivities of those with offensive opinions. I agree with those who say that we should not respect the sensibilities of those who think that someone should be killed for writing a novel or drawing a cartoon, no matter how much they may be offended by these things. We should not respect these views because they are not worthy of respect. But you can tolerate people without respecting their opinions.

The upshot of the previous discussion is that tolerance is not the mistaken view that "anything goes," that all opinions are as good as all others. This is an incorrect theoretical view about the truth or correctness of opinions. But tolerance, as I understand it, is a *practical* attitude toward the *holders* of these opinions. It involves allowing people to live with their opinions, for the most part, and with behavior based on those opinions. Outside the context of education, we do not have any general obligation to change the opinions of others; and within certain limits, we do not have any obligation to interfere with the behavior of others either.

But within what limits? What limits does tolerance actually imply? When should we stop tolerating the behavior of others? A sensible doctrine of tolerance should not imply, absurdly, that we should allow any behavior whatsoever from those with whom we differ. It must be possible to be a tolerant person yet not tolerate offensive behavior. A belief in tolerance is, in this respect, like a belief in free speech or democracy. A sensible doctrine of free speech should not imply (say) that the continuous broadcasting of obscenities in public places should be permitted. And a sensible belief in democracy should not imply (say) that all decisions made by governments should be validated by a popular vote. Just as one can believe in a principle of free speech while believing that some speech should be banned, so one can believe in democracy while believing that governments may make decisions on behalf of the people that the people do not need to validate (and that they might even reject if asked). Similarly with tolerance. Atheists can—and should—tolerate a wide range of religious behavior of which they do not approve, and indirectly the religious beliefs to which they give rise, without thinking that they should allow them all.

But what do we mean by "allowing" certain kinds of behavior? One answer appeals to legal and political prohibition. We should not tolerate behavior that is against the rule of law, so long as the rule of law is reasonably formulated and coherent. Which behavior should be prohibited by law may be clear in extreme cases—murder and female genital mutilation are obvious examples—and less clear at the margins. The difficult job, as always, is deciding which lines to draw and where exactly to draw them; and I have nothing new to say here on these difficult questions of detail. But no one should be in doubt that a line should be drawn: it seems to me that work on the extent to which secular or predominantly a-religious liberal states can incorporate religious behavior should surely be one of the most pressing tasks for liberal political philosophy.

My concern here, however, is not with politics and the law but with how we atheists might implement toleration in our lives as individuals. In our individual lives, the question of which things to tolerate is in a certain sense easier and in a certain sense more difficult than in the political and legal contexts. It is easier because if someone is breaking the law, then we have no obligation to tolerate them (unless the law is badly motivated, badly formulated, trivial, or immoral, of course). But it is also more difficult to know what to do when we encounter religious behavior that is not illegal but nonetheless objectionable. In the last few pages of this book I will make some remarks on this, and I will try to draw some general morals.

Let's return to the question of respect. In a valuable discussion of this question, Simon Blackburn talks about an experience he had when he was invited to dinner by Jewish colleagues and asked to participate in some ritual. He does not say exactly what the ritual was, but it was clearly something undemanding and relatively trivial ("put on a hat, or some such"). He declined to do this, and when it was explained to him that he was merely being asked to show respect for his hosts' views, he said he could not do it even for that reason. "The evening" he reports, "was strained after that."[10]

Blackburn's vignette raises interesting questions for those who believe in tolerance of religious practices. On the one hand, I agree with Blackburn that we should not respect all those views with which we disagree. We can respect those who hold the view, in the abstract moral sense described previously, and we should not object to them holding their rituals, so long as these rituals involve nothing morally offensive; but we surely have no obligation deriving from any principle of tolerance to respect their views. And the hosts' insistence that Blackburn respect these views by participating in the ritual seems inconsiderate and even intrusive. On the other hand, there is something churlish about refusing to go along with an undemanding expression of what is, after all, from your point of view, a wholly false or even nonsensical belief. What harm would be done, on this occasion, by going along with it in a spirit of friendship, or at least civility? Is the value of publicly declaring your own integrity and lack of hypocrisy something that so obviously trumps the disvalue of spoiling a social occasion? This might be ultimately a matter of taste, and different people's tastes fall out differently.

The example might suggest that the issue is simply about mere politeness and social niceties. But things look slightly different when we consider a more serious religious ritual. To draw on an experience of my own: Some years ago I found myself at the Jewish funeral of a colleague and acquaintance who died suddenly in middle age and good health. The funeral, held a day or so after the death as is traditional, was raw with sorrow, and it was attended by Jews and non-Jews. At one point in the ceremony someone passed around a bag of skullcaps, and everyone who was not already wearing one took one and put it on. There were at least a hundred people there. Like the rest, I put on the skullcap and felt no awkwardness or incongruity in doing so. But would it have been better to politely refuse the skullcap on the grounds that it is wrong to go along with a practice "that might be the expression of a belief that I do not hold," in Blackburn's words?[11] I suspect that many atheists would not insist on this in a context like a funeral. To insist on only acting in conformity with your rather abstract beliefs is not just a failure of politeness, it can be a failure of sensitivity to things that are much more important than one's own integrity as an inquirer. This occasion wasn't about me or my atheistical beliefs but rather about the mystery and sadness of an early death, and the acknowledgment of one's community and common humanity with the mourners.

But there will also be cases in which speaking up for what one believes is consistent with a properly tolerant attitude. If a religion requires that women are not allowed to do certain things simply because they are women—for example, be priests or bishops in a church—then feminists will want to object to this view because it demeans women, treats them as in some way second-rate, and denies them the opportunities for spiritual fulfillment that men have. Objecting to this need not involve interfering with their practices, which may not in any case be possible or practical. But tolerance need not require that one endure in silence those views one finds unacceptable.

There are occasions, then, when a tolerant person can legitimately object to the religious beliefs of others, even while tolerating their behavior. Should one attempt to change those beliefs? And if so, how? What seems plain to me is that the way *not* to do this is to point out that these beliefs belong to an unscientific or outmoded cosmology or worldview. This is unlikely to have any good effect. Those, like many scholars and academics, who live their life in the pursuit of theoretical or factual truth tend to overestimate both the efficacy and the value of pointing out to people that they are wrong. When allied with the New Atheists' views about the nature of religion and its role in the problems of the world, this can result in attempts to use one's intellectual abilities to enter into the debate about religion by showing the religious why their views are irrational; based on fallacious reasoning, indoctrination, or the remnants of ancient superstitions; or all of these.

And yet these attempts rarely succeed. The New Atheists do claim the occasional convert, and their books have undeniably given succor to some of those who have felt their lives blighted by religion in various ways. But—to repeat my point again—their arguments do not touch the vast majority of believers, and they are dismissed by scholars of religion as missing the point. Of course, it is always possible to accuse these scholars of self-deception, and the believers of ignorance or irrationality, but the failure of engagement on both sides is quite striking. The religious do not recognize themselves in the New Atheists' descriptions, and the New Atheists can give no account of why this is so, other than the persistent irrationality of the religious and so on. Their objections to religion therefore come across as a kind of moralizing, in the sense of making "a moral judgment in an inappropriate context, that is, propounding it in a context or in a way which seems to ascribe to it too much of the wrong kind of weight or effectiveness," to borrow Raymond Geuss's words.[12]

The account of religion that I have sketched in this book explains why it is so hard for the New Atheists to get the religious to listen to them. It is because their conception of religious belief is so deeply mistaken. I have sketched a picture of religion in terms of the combination of two ideas, the religious impulse and identification, and the link between them provided by the idea of the sacred. None of these ideas fits the New Atheist picture of religion as a kind of proto-scientific theory, or as a proto-scientific theory plus a moral code. It is because the New Atheists fail to see the heart of religion that they are unable to engage with their opponents in any intelligible way.

But if the New Atheists had a more accurate conception of religion, then they would need different arguments against it. If the content of the religious impulse is not like an empirical, scientific hypothesis, then arguments that show that religious beliefs fare badly in their explanatory power as hypotheses will not have much traction. If it is not true that there is some straightforward correlation or connection between violence, atrocity, irrationality, and religious belief, or if it is true (which it surely is) that the vast majority of the billions of religious people in the world are repelled by the violence of the tiny minority, then few will be moved by the arguments of Richard Dawkins, Christopher Hitchens, and others that it is religion—rather than psychological disturbance, poverty, exploitation, nationalist aggression, globalization, or any number of other complex factors—that is the cause of their problems.

The proposal that we approach religion with tolerance and the attempt at understanding should not be taken to express a complacency about our current situation. On the contrary: the "way of tolerance" seems to me a more realistic view of the prospects for atheism than (what we might call) the New Atheists' "way of conversion." Clearly the world faces enormous challenges, some of which have strong connections to dominant religious traditions. But theorizing about our attitude to religion is useless unless it is actually applicable to the actual concrete situation we find ourselves in. This is why we need a proper understanding of the nature of religious belief, a proper sense of what can realistically be achieved to make things better, and how this might be done.

Looked at in this way, the New Atheists' campaign against religion seems excessively optimistic and idealistic. Religious belief is very unlikely to be removed by scientific evidence, and its waxing and waning in certain parts of the world are the result of contingent cultural traditions and political factors that often have little to do with rational argument. Contrary to what some atheists think, religion does not always decline when people become more educated. The United States has the most sophisticated and well-endowed system of higher education in the world, yet religion (largely Christianity) thrives there as it does in some of the poorest parts of the world. And you still find believers among the highly educated products of American universities—even among their scientists and philosophers—as you do among those who have learned little science. The optimistic view that religion will wither away in the face of science and reason does not have the facts on its side.

This optimistic view may derive from a desire to teach people the truth, or from the belief that it is always better for people to know the truth rather than not. It's hard to deny the appeal of this ideal. How can any serious intellectual or teacher hold that it would be better for someone to live in falsehood? But, of course, the practical value of any such ideal depends on to what extent it can actually be attained. And whether it can be attained depends not only on the receptiveness of others to having their minds changed but also on the availability of a channel of communication in which alternative views to theirs can be expressed. In much of the world there are no such channels, and there is a vast lack of receptivity to having one's mind changed away from religion. This is one reason why I say that the New Atheist view is optimistic and idealistic.

By contrast, the way of tolerance is a more realistic (and therefore pessimistic) response to the reality of religion, and of human nature, than the idealistic optimism of the New Atheists. Atheists are not going to eliminate religion, either through legislation or through rational argument. The problems the world is facing are practical political problems, problems whose solutions need cooperation, coordination, and compromise. Any view about how atheists and theists should live together and interact must ultimately confront the fact that neither religion nor secularism is going to disappear. The least we can hope for is peaceful coexistence, while the most we can hope for is a kind of dialogue between those who hold very different views of reality. A genuine dialogue of this kind will be very difficult to achieve, but the first step must be for each side to gain an adequate understanding of the views of the other.

Notes

PREFACE

1. John Gray, *Black Mass* (London: Allen Lane, 2007), 208.

1. RELIGION AND THE ATHEIST'S POINT OF VIEW

1. Pew Research Center, "The Global Religious Landscape," December 18, 2012, http://www.pewforum.org/2012/12/18/global-religious-landscape-exec/.
2. Friedrich Nietzsche, *On the Genealogy of Morality,* ed. Keith Ansell-Pearson, trans. Carol Diethe

(1887; repr., Cambridge: Cambridge University Press, 2007), 53.

3. Émile Durkheim, *The Elementary Forms of Religious Life* (1912; repr., Oxford: Oxford University Press, 2001), 5.

4. William James, *The Varieties of Religious Experience* (New York: Longmans, Green, 1902), 26.

5. Karen Armstrong, *Fields of Blood* (London: Bodley Head, 2014), 2.

6. James, *The Varieties of Religious Experience,* 26.

7. James Tartaglia, *Philosophy in a Meaningless Life* (London: Bloomsbury, 2015).

8. Simon Blackburn, interview by Rick Lewis, *Philosophy Now,* no. 99 (November / December 2013), https://philosophynow.org/issues/99/Simon_Blackburn.

9. Armstrong, *Fields of Blood,* 3.

10. The phrase is from A. W. Moore, *The Evolution of Modern Metaphysics: Making Sense of Things* (Cambridge: Cambridge University Press, 2012).

11. Thomas Nagel, *Secular Philosophy and the Religious Temperament* (Oxford: Oxford University Press, 2010), 5.

12. Ibid., 6.

13. John Cottingham, *The Meaning of Life* (London: Routledge, 2003), 100.

14. Durkheim, *The Elementary Forms of Religious Life,* 28.

15. Daniel C. Dennett, *Breaking the Spell* (London: Allen Lane, 2006), 9.

16. A. C. Grayling, *Against All Gods* (London: Oberon Books, 2007), 29.

17. Richard Dawkins, *The God Delusion* (London: Bantam, 2006), 52.

18. Pascal Boyer, *Religion Explained* (New York: Basic Books, 2001), 10.

19. Durkheim, *The Elementary Forms of Religious Life,* 32; see also Boyer, *Religion Explained,* 7.

20. Louise Antony, ed., *Philosophers without Gods* (Oxford: Oxford University Press, 2007), back cover.

21. Julian Baggini, *Atheism: A Very Short Introduction* (Oxford: Oxford University Press, 2003), 10.

22. David Bentley Hart, *Atheist Delusions* (New Haven, CT: Yale University Press, 2009), 11.

23. 1 Cor. 15:14.

24. Ronald Dworkin, *Religion without God* (Cambridge, MA: Harvard University Press, 2013), 1–2.

25. Alain de Botton, *Religion for Atheists* (London: Penguin, 2012), 17.

26. Dawkins, *The God Delusion,* 262.

27. American Humanist Association, "Humanist Manifesto I," 1933, http://americanhumanist.org /Humanism/Humanist_Manifesto_I.

28. See the history of the South Place Ethical Society in London, for example: http://conwayhall.org.uk /ethical-society/beginnings/.

29. John Gray, *Gray's Anatomy* (London: Allen Lane, 2009), 15.

30. Richard Dawkins, "The Future Looks Bright," *Guardian,* June 21, 2003, http://www.theguardian .com/books/2003/jun/21/society.richarddawkins.

31. Richard Norman, *On Humanism* (London: Routledge, 2004), 26.

32. Bylaw of the International Humanist and Ethical Union no. 2, http://iheu.org/humanism/what-is -humanism/.

33. Norman, *On Humanism,* 24.

34. John Gray, *Black Mass* (London: Allen Lane, 2007), 189.

35. Derek C. Penn, Keith J. Holyoak, and Daniel J. Povinelli, "Darwin's Mistake: Explaining the Discontinuity between Human and Nonhuman Minds," *Behavioral and Brain Sciences* 31 (2008): 109.

36. Jeremy Bentham, *An Introduction to the Principles of Morals and Legislation,* ed. J. H. Burns and H. L. A. Hart (1789; repr., Oxford: Clarendon Press, 1970), 283n.

2. THE RELIGIOUS IMPULSE

1. William James, *The Varieties of Religious Experience* (New York: Longmans, Green, 1902), 53.

2. Simon Blackburn, interview by Rick Lewis, *Philosophy Now,* no. 99 (November/December 2013), https://philosophynow.org/issues/99/Simon _Blackburn.

3. George Herbert, "The Elixir," in *The Complete English Poems* (London: Penguin, 2005), 174.

4. Max Weber, "Science as a Vocation" (1919), in Weber, *The Vocation Lectures,* ed. David Owen and Tracy B. Strong, trans. Rodney Livingstone (Indianapolis: Hackett, 2004), 13.

5. Philip Larkin, "Aubade," in *Collected Poems,* edited by Anthony Thwaite (London: Faber and Faber, 2003), 208.

6. Kenneth Taylor, "Without the Net of Providence: Atheism and the Human Adventure," in *Philosophers without Gods,* ed. Louise Antony (Oxford: Oxford University Press, 2007), 150.

7. Larkin, "Aubade." 208.

8. Thomas Nagel, *Secular Philosophy and the Religious Temperament* (Oxford: Oxford University Press, 2010), 8.

9. Weber, "Science as a Vocation," 12.

10. See, for example, Justin L. Barrett, "Exploring the Natural Foundations of Religion," *Trends in Cognitive Science* 4, no. 1 (2000): 29–34.

11. James, *The Varieties of Religious Experience,* 27.

12. Nagel, *Secular Philosophy and the Religious Temperament,* 6.

13. John Gray, *Gray's Anatomy* (London: Allen Lane, 2009), 15.

14. Richard Dawkins, *The God Delusion* (London: Bantam, 2006), 52.

15. Christopher Hitchens, *God Is Not Great: How Religion Poisons Everything* (New York: Twelve, 2007), 66–67.

16. Dawkins, *The God Delusion,* 52.

17. Richard Dawkins, "When Religion Steps on Science's Turf," *Free Inquiry* 18, no. 2 (1998), http://pds4.egloos.com/pds/200709/04/59/Richard _Dawkins_-_When_Religion_Steps_On_Sciences _Turf.pdf.

18. Stephen Jay Gould, *Rocks of Ages: Science and Religion in the Fullness of Life* (New York: Ballantine Books, 2002), 5.

19. Francis Spufford, *Unapologetic: Why, Despite Everything, Christianity Can Still Make Surprising Emotional Sense* (London: Faber and Faber, 2013), 68.

20. Søren Kirkegaard, *Concluding Unscientific Postscript,* ed. Alastair Hannay (1846; repr., Cambridge: Cambridge University Press, 2009), 171; emphasis added.

21. John D. Caputo, *Truth: Philosophy in Transit* (London: Penguin, 2013), 49.

22. Philip Kitcher, *Life after Faith* (New Haven, CT: Yale University Press, 2014), 103.

23. Alfred North Whitehead, *Science and the Modern World* (1925; repr., New York: Free Press, 1967), 192.

3. IDENTIFICATION

1. Daniel C. Dennett, *Breaking the Spell* (London: Allen Lane, 2006), 9.

2. Ronald Dworkin, *Religion without God* (Cambridge, MA: Harvard University Press, 2013), 23.

3. Émile Durkheim, *The Elementary Forms of Religious Life* (1912; repr., Oxford: Oxford University Press, 2001), 42.

4. Ibid., 43.

5. Pascal Boyer, *Religion Explained* (New York: Basic Books, 2001), 6–9.

6. Roger Scruton, *The Soul of the World* (Edinburgh: Edinburgh University Press, 2014), 14.

7. Martin Heidegger, *Being and Time,* trans. John Macquarrie and Edward Robinson (1927; repr., London: SCM Press, 1962), Division 1, chapter 5, §38.

8. John Rawls, *A Theory of Justice* (Cambridge, MA: Belknap Press of Harvard University Press, 1971), 74.

9. A. C. Grayling, *Against All Gods* (London: Oberon Books, 2007), 10. Richard Dawkins makes the same point in *The God Delusion* (London: Bantam, 2006), 296.

10. Richard Dawkins, *Unweaving the Rainbow* (1998; repr., London: Penguin, 2006), x.

11. Philip Kitcher, *Life after Faith* (New Haven, CT: Yale University Press, 2014), 120.

12. Durkheim, *The Elementary Forms of Religious Life,* 46.

13. Ibid., 34.

14. Ibid., 46.

15. Scruton, *The Soul of the World,* 15.

16. Karen Armstrong, *Fields of Blood* (London: Bodley Head, 2014), 2.

17. Scruton, *The Soul of the World,* 15.

18. Hugh Trevor-Roper, *One Hundred Letters from Hugh Trevor-Roper,* ed. Richard Davenport-Hines (Oxford: Oxford University Press, 2014), 349.

19. Durkheim, *The Elementary Forms of Religious Life,* 45.

20. Ibid., 43.

21. See, for example, the essays in Ben Rogers, ed., *Is Nothing Sacred?* (London: Routledge, 2004).

22. Simon Blackburn, "Religion and Respect," in *Philosophers without Gods,* ed. Louise Antony (Oxford: Oxford University Press, 2007), 191.

4. RELIGION AND VIOLENCE

1. Richard Dawkins, *The God Delusion* (London: Bantam, 2006), 43.
2. Ibid.
3. Christopher Hitchens, *God Is Not Great: How Religion Poisons Everything* (New York: Twelve, 2007), 18–21.
4. See Karen Armstrong, *Fields of Blood: Religion and the History of Violence* (London: Bodley Head, 2014), especially 10–11.
5. Ibid., 25.
6. Sam Harris, *The End of Faith* (New York: Norton, 2004), 12.
7. Ibid., 79.
8. John Gray, *Gray's Anatomy* (London: Allen Lane, 2009), 3.
9. Harris, *The End of Faith,* 27.
10. Ramachandra Guha, *India after Gandhi* (Oxford: Oxford University Press, 2007).
11. Hitchens, *God Is Not Great,* 18.
12. Dawkins, *The God Delusion,* 43.
13. Voltaire, *Questions sur les miracles, à M. Claparede, Professeur de théologie à Genève, par un proposant: Ou extrait de diverses lettres de M. de Voltaire, avec les réponses par M. Néedham* (1765, repr., Farmington

Hills, MI: Gale ECCO Print Editions, 2010), 72. Voltaire actually wrote, "Certainement qui est en droit de vous rendre absurde est en droit de vous rendre injuste," which can be translated as "Certainly, whoever can make you absurd can also make you unjust." This is a slightly different point from that made in the usual translation.

14. Harris, *The End of Faith,* 232.

15. Ibid., 85.

16. T. M. Scanlon, *What We Owe to Each Other* (Cambridge, MA: Harvard University Press, 1998), 17.

17. Anthony Kenny, *The God of the Philosophers* (Oxford: Oxford University Press, 1979), 129.

5. THE MEANING OF TOLERANCE

1. For the 2006 figure, see see John Micklethwait and Adrian Woolridge, *God Is Back* (New York: Penguin, 2009), 5. For the number of Christians in China, see Pew Research Center, "Appendix C: Methodology for China," http://www.pewforum .org/files/2011/12/ChristianityAppendixC.pdf, in *Global Christianity: A Report on the Size and Distribution of the World's Christian Population*, December 19, 2011, http://www.pewforum.org /files/2011/12/Christianity-fullreport-web.pdf.

2. John Gray, *Black Mass* (London: Allen Lane, 2007), 207.

3. Ibid.

4. Brian Leiter, *Why Tolerate Religion?* (Princeton, NJ: Princeton University Press, 2013).

5. David Lewis, "Mill and Milquetoast," *Australasian Journal of Philosophy* 67 (1989): 152–171, 152.

6. W. V. Quine, *Word and Object* (Cambridge, MA: MIT Press, 1960), 59.

7. Susan Mendus, "My Brother's Keeper: The Politics of Intolerance," in *The Politics of Toleration* (Edinburgh: Edinburgh University Press, 1999), 3.

8. Tariq Ramadan, *The Quest for Meaning* (Harmondsworth, UK: Penguin, 2010), 48.

9. Frank Furedi, *On Tolerance* (London: Continuum, 2011).

10. Simon Blackburn, "Religion and Respect," in *Philosophers without Gods,* ed. Louise Antony (Oxford: Oxford University Press, 2007), 179.

11. Ibid.

12. Raymond Geuss, *Reality and Its Dreams* (Cambridge, MA: Harvard University Press, 2016), 96.

Index